Generis
PUBLISHING

Fr. Laurien Nyiribakwe, S.J

FAITH-HEALING MINISTRY IN AFRICA

A CATHOLIC BIO-SOCIAL ETHICS

And He could do no miracle there except that He laid His hands on a few sick people and healed them. Mark 6:5.

Copyright © 2021 Laurien Nyiribakwe, S.J
Copyright © 2021 Generis Publishing

All rights reserved. This book or any portion thereof may not be reproduced or used in any manner whatsoever without the written permission of the publisher except for the use of brief quotations in a book review.

Title: FAITH-HEALING MINISTRY IN AFRICA
A CATHOLIC BIO-SOCIAL ETHICS

Author: Fr. Laurien Nyiribakwe, S.J

ISBN: 978-1-63902-448-3

Cover image: www.pixabay.com

Publisher: Generis Publishing
Online orders: www.generis-publishing.com
Contact email: info@generis-publishing.com

TABLE OF CONTENTS

- SUMMARY 6
- PREAMBLE 7
- ACKNOWLEDGMENTS 8
- GENERAL INTRODUCTION 9
- TERMS AND CONTEXT 10
- CHAPTER I 15
- THE AFRICAN WORLDVIEW AND THE SEARCH FOR SPIRITUAL POWERS ... 15
  - 1.1. AN AFRICAN WORLDVIEW AND SPIRITUAL HEALING 21
  - 1.2. AFRICAN TRADITIONAL RELIGION (ATR) AND HEALERS 27
  - 1.3. LYANGOMBE AS A HEALER AMONG BANYARWANDA 30
  - 1.4. CHRISTIANITY AND SPIRITUAL HEALING POWERS 38
  - 1.5. LOOKING FOR A REALISTIC APPROACH 44
- CONCLUSION 46
- CHAPTER II 48
- FAITH-HEALING IN SUB-SAHARAN AFRICA 48
  - 2.1. WHY IS FAITH HEALING IMPORTANT IN AFRICAN SOCIETY? 48
  - 2.2. CATHOLIC FAITH-HEALING: MAJOR DEVELOPMENTS 50
  - 2.3. HEALING IN AFRICAN CATHOLIC CHRISTIANITY 55
    - 2.3.1. Meinrad Pierre Hebga in Cameroon (1923-2008 56
    - 2.3.2. Emmanuel Milingo in Zambia (1930-) 59
    - 2.3.3. Fr. Léopold Mvukiye (b.1954- in Burundi) 59
    - 2.3.4. Fr. Ubald Rugirangoga (b.1956-d.2021 in Rwanda) 64
- OVERALL CONCLUDING REMARKS 69
- CHAPTER III 73
- TOWARD AN EFFECTIVE FAITH-HEALING MINISTRY 73
  - 3.1. THE CLAIM FOR HEALING MINISTRY 73
    - 3.1.1. Diabolic possession 74
    - 3.1.2. Evil vexation. 75
    - 3.1.3. Diabolical obsession. 75
    - 3.1.4. Hostility towards divine values 75
  - 3.2. CRITERIA OF DISCERNMENT 78
    - 3.2.1. The Preferential Option for The Poor. 78
    - 3.2.2. The Art of Accompaniment. 82
    - 3.3.3. A Multi-sectorial and Bio-ethical Perspective: 85
    - 3.3.4. Doctrinal and Pastoral Discernment, ... 89
- CONCLUSION 91
  - GENERAL CONCLUSION 93
- REFERENCES 96

SUMMARY

The present book engages three fields; namely, African traditional religion (ATR), Catholic religion and biomedical sciences in their endeavor to sustain health and well-being. It proceeds from the conviction that faith-healing is an essential element of theological bioethics. The discipline of theological bioethics reflects on the questions that arise in medicine and treatment of illness, and issues related to human biology, decisions to be made in case of this or that pain or disease, including the discernment on the normal and paranormal phenomena that could affect people of faith. The search for spiritual powers, as they are related to the not-yet-born, to the living, and to the dead is a crucial question to Catholic bioethics and pastoral ministry. This work considers that complex issue without pretending to offer a definitive answer. It relies on Catholic bioethics as a multi-disciplinary approach illumined by faith to propose some criteria for making a discernment regarding powers of spiritual healing which are claimed in today's Christian Sub-Saharan Africa.

PREAMBLE

Better a poor man strong and robust, than a rich man with wasted frame. More precious than gold is health and well-being, contentment of spirit than coral. No treasure greater than a healthy body; no happiness, than a joyful heart! Preferable is death to a bitter life, unending sleep to constant illness. Dainties set before one who cannot eat are like the offerings placed before a tomb. What good is an offering to an idol that can neither taste nor smell? So, it is with the afflicted man who groans at the good things his eyes behold.

(Sirach 30:14-20)

Hold the physician in honor, for he is essential to you, and God it was who established his profession. From God the doctor has his wisdom...His knowledge makes the doctor distinguished... [But God] endows men with the knowledge to glory in His mighty works, through which the doctor eases pain and the druggist prepares his medicines; thus, God's creative work continues without cease in its efficacy on the... earth...The doctor beseeches God that his diagnosis may be correct, and his treatment bring about a cure.

(Sirach 38:1-3, 6-8, 14)

ACKNOWLEDGMENTS

The grace of God was poured out on me abundantly (1Tim 1:14). May the name of the Lord be praised, above all.

The publication of the present book would not have been realized without unceasing generosity and support of my professors and colleagues. Among them I would like to name my professors and mentors in the School of Theology and Ministry of Boston College: Lisa Sowle Cahill, Ph.D.; and Sr. Margaret Eletta Guider, Th.D. I want also to express my heartfelt gratitude to many Jesuit companions who supported and encouraged me to speak to the world through this book, in particular: Fr. Augustin Some S.J, Fr. Sané Médard Barwendé, S.J; Fr. Simon Smith S.J. and Fr. Matthew Baugh S.J.

This book advocates on the behalf of the sick, the biologically, socially, and psychologically broken. The book raises the voice of the disabled, resonates the battles of the healers and exorcists in Sub-Saharan Africa, as it resists spiritualism and fideism. This book is an instrument of promotion of health in Africa, especially amid the forgotten and the crucified by individual and social ills. The author calls for an intellectual sensitivity and discernment enlighten by faith in action.

General Introduction

This present book is articulated in three parts. The first part describes the African worldview, demonstrating that African Christianity and Western medicine exist on a profound terrain of belief in spiritual powers. The second part investigates Catholic teaching about faith-healing powers and its development before and after the Second Vatican Council (1962). I illustrate the rise of Catholic faith-healing ministry in Sub-Saharan Africa, pointing out the underlying social problems as a call to pastoral and ethical approaches. The third part highlights criteria of discernment for an effective faith-healing ministry in Africa through the lens of Catholic social teaching.

This book attempts to reply to the prevailing question: Could there be criteria for an effective faith-healing ministry in Africa, as seen through the lens of Catholic ethics? I argue that a Catholic faith-healing ministry could be effective if it is, 1) rooted in the preferential option for the poor, 2) not antagonistic to conventional medicine, 2) accompanying the sick, the psychologically, physically, and spiritually ill; 3) enhancing theological biosocial approaches. I assert that the healing ministry in Africa needs to be deeply discerned and conventional medicine to be upgraded and so effectively tackle the issues of the suffering and sickness in the Sub-Saharan region.

Terms and Context

Different scholars attempt to define faith-healing in a variety of ways. The Harper Collins' *Dictionary of Religion* defines faith-healing as "a Christian practice of restoring health by means of prayer," and broadly as "transfer of divine power, or the intervention of the Holy Spirit."[1] This definition corresponds to the definition given in *The Our Sunday's Visitor's Catholic Encyclopedia* which considers faith-healing or divine faith cure as "a relatively recent phenomenon within the history of Christianity. Faith-healing refers to two elements:

> A group of believers with kind of praying, believing that all diseases can be cured by God's intervention in connection with prayers of deep faith form part of healing movement. The prayer of faith includes taking authority over whatever illness is present, casting it out or addressing it, invoking the blood of Christ (or his stripes or his cross), and claiming the act of faith and healing process to be under God's sovereign rule.[2]

Throughout centuries, the Roman Catholic Church has seen many faith-healing followers. Some are officially recognized by the Church after scientific and theological investigations, others remain unlikely. The Church emphasizes on the natural means of healing without excluding the possibility of supernatural healing. In the *Instructions on Prayers for Healing*, the Congregation of the Doctrine of Faith [CDF] states:

> There is abundant witness throughout the Church history to healings connected with places of prayer sanctuaries, in the presence of the relics of martyrs or another saint. The same also happens today at Lourdes, ... Such healings, however, do not imply a charism of healing because they are not connected with a person who has such a charism, but they need to be considered when we evaluate the above-mentioned prayer meetings from a doctrinal perspective.[3]

---

[1] Jonathan Z. Smith, William Scott Green, eds. *The Harper Collins Dictionary of Religion* (San Francisco, CA: Harper Collins Publishers, 1995), 355.

[2] *Our Sunday's Visitor Catholic Encyclopedia,* Peter M.J. Stravinskas, ed. (Huntington, IN: Our Sunday's Visitors Publishers, 1998), 415.

[3] The Congregation of the Doctrine of Faith, *The Instruction on Prayers for Healing, September 14,* 2000), I.

Upholding the priority put on scientific means of healing, the CDF notes:

> Obviously, recourse to prayer does not exclude, but rather encourages the use of effective natural means for preserving and restoring health, as well as leading the Church's sons and daughters to care for the sick, to assist them in body and spirit, and to seek to cure disease. Indeed, part of the plan laid out in God's providence is that we should fight strenuously against all sickness and carefully seek the blessings of good health.[4]

Despite significant improvement in medicine and biotechnologies and the church endeavors to promote health and fight against diseases, the sub-Saharan health context is alarming. Healthcare providers in Sub-Saharan Africa struggle with a lack of robust medical infrastructure and its maintenance, availability, and accessibility of health systems especially in rural areas, adequate funding, and responsible public administration, among other problems. Writing from South Africa, one of the richest countries in Africa, Dave Puo observes: "when you seek medical attention, you are informed that there is no medication and advised to go to the big hospitals,"[5] where poor people cannot financially afford healthcare, especially when they suffer from chronic diseases and disabilities. Such a complaint reveals millions of sick people on throughout the continent in search of medical care and in need of healing.

It is arguable that conventional medicine offers tremendous hope to Africans in preventing and curing diseases, yet it falls short of meeting the profound need of Africans that African ethics requires. Indeed, the African ethics sees a person in relation with others. As Bénézet Bujo asserts, the Western ethics stresses the individual while African ethics is communitarian. The African person belongs to a community, to a certain lineage, he/she is associated with the not-yet born, the living, the ancestors and God.[6] In this view, African ethics upholds the World Health Organization's definition of health as "a state of complete, physical, mental, and social well-being, and not merely absence of diseases or infirmity."[7] According to Jean Marc Ela's *My Faith as an African*, health comes first for most Africans. It takes family, job

---

[4] Ibid., II.

[5] Dave Puo as cited by Tefo Pheage "Dying from Lack of Medicines" *African Renewal*. December - March 2017. Online https://www.un.org/africarenewal/magazine/december-2016-march-2017/dying-lack-medicines. Accessed on November 10th, 2018.

[6] Benezet Bujo, *Foundations of an African Ethics: Beyond the Universal Claims of Western Morality*, tans. Brian McNeil (New York: The Crossroad, 2001), 2.

[7] World Health Organization, https://www.who.int/about/who-we-are/constitution. Accessed on November, 2018.

and wealth.[8] Health is sacred. The Yoruba people in Nigeria rightly say: "Health is everything, health is wealth, whoever has good health has everything."[9] Health is a gift from the Supreme Being, the Creator. Thus, it needs to be preserved by all possible means, with respect to God, in good relations with ourselves, in fellowship with others, and by caring for the whole creation.

Before the advent of conventional medicine to the continent, Africans relied on supernatural powers, on the power of nature and traditional healing. In his book, *Medicine and Religion: A Historical Introduction,* Gary B. Ferngreen describes Egyptian prehistory, an uncovering of the belief in magic and in divine power as a part of the human search for answers to sickness and suffering. In Ferngreen's words: "In case of injury one might turn to the supernatural in seeking to understand why an accident occurred."[10] The Egyptians associated sickness to disharmony with deities but did not know the spiritual cause of disease.[11] Egyptians also believed God imparts powers to natural beings such as the "*pharaoh.*" The goal was to live in "constant serenity" and "happy resignation" to the supernatural order, because "with the *pharaoh* as god, the divine order (*ma'at*) was always knowable."[12] This kind of belief was "naturalistic and polytheistic." For Egyptians, the power of deities was at work in the *cosmos.*[13] The causal agents of health and disease were taken as "gods, ghosts of dead persons, and demons.[14]

While today's science-imbued mind may not understand or disregard the beliefs described above, many Africans think sickness and diseases come from external factors including sorcerers, malevolent forces, and evil spirits. As Esther E. Acolatse maintains, beliefs in spiritual powers and their impact on human life, "has not changed, diminished or shifted over time, despite modern technology."[15]

Some scholars saw African belief as henotheistic rather than polytheistic. Henotheism is a belief system which holds the existence of one God as the supreme being without denying the existence of multiple deities around God.

---

[8] Jean Marc Ela, *My Faith as An African,* Paris, Karthala, 1985, 95.

[9] Dorcas Olupande Akintunde "Women as Healers," *African Women, Religion, and Health,* Isabel Apawo Phiri, Sorojini Nadar (Maryknoll, NY: Orbis Book, 2006), 159.

[10] Gary B. Ferngreen, *Medicine & Religion*: A Historical Introduction. John Hopkins University Press, 2014), 15.

[11] Gary Ferngreen, *Medicine and Religion*, 16.

[12] Ibid.

[13] Ibid, 15.

[14] Ibid.

[15] Esther R. Acolatse, *Powers and Principalities: Biblical Realism in Africa and the West* (Grand Rapids, Mi: Williams B. Eedermans, 2018), 3.

Besides belief in spiritual beings, Africans believed ancestors as connectors of the living to the Supreme Being, as providers of life and health on earth. Thus, Africans implore the spirits of their ancestors by the help of *"nga'nga"* (traditional healers), who are agents between the visible world and the invisible world, the world of God, ancestors, and spirits. Eric de Rosny, a French Jesuit priest, in his book *Healers in the Night*, lived with the *"nga'nga"* of Douala in Cameroon. These "masters of the night" opened his eyes to the "World of Spirits."[16] His work seeks "to throw light on the mysterious affinity between human beings living at one another's cultural antipode."[17] Kabiro wa Gatumu admits, "belief in ghosts perseveres in modern Africa despite the influx of modern technology and scientific knowledge."[18] Kwame Anthony Appiah adds: "In cultures all over the continent of Africa, the notion that a supreme Being (God) created the universe and that disembodied, invisible spirits affect, and often control the physical world is uncontroversial and need not be rationally defended."[19] This conviction follows John Mbiti's study of three hundred different African peoples, unveiling "myriad of spirits… reported from every African people."[20] Mbiti admits: "whatever science may do to prove the existence or non-existence of the spirits, one thing remains undeniable, namely that for African peoples the spirits are a reality and a reality which must be considered whether it is clear, blurred or confused."[21] Those who are sick look for priests in search of a better life, while others relate death with the actions of evil spirits or witchcraft.[22] Christian mission in Africa has opposed belief in spiritual powers of traditional religion, calling for faith in the power of Christ.

Nowadays, in many regions of Sub-Saharan Africa, Christian religious traditions and beliefs have replaced those of African religions on both practical and doctrinal levels. Also, Christianity largely has contributed to the improvement of medical care in Africa. Yet recourse to traditional healing and belief in supernatural powers remains prevalent.

Faith-healing according to clergy and laypersons is claimed to compensate for the failure or lack of access to conventional medicine, yet

---

[16] See Eric de Rosny, S.J. *Healers in the Night*. Trans. Robert R. Barr (Maryknol: New York, 1985), preface.
[17] Ibid.
[18] Kabiro wa Gatumu, *The Pauline Concept of Supernatural Powers: Reading from the African Wordview* (Eugene, OR: Wipf & Stock Publishers, 2009), 15.
[19] Kwame Anthony Appiah, *My Father's House: Africa in Philosophy of Culture* (Oxford: Oxford University Press, 1992), 118.
[20] John S. Mbiti, *African Religion and Philosophy* (Oxford: Heinemann, 1990), 29.
[21] Ibid., 89.
[22] Ibid.

authentic healing must be evaluated both through the lens of Catholic ethics and modern progress in medicine, in biotechnology, in psychiatry, and other social and scientific disciplines. I am persuaded by the claim that Catholic theology could help us reflect anew on the meaning of the healing powers given to certain Christians in a way that could preserve traditional African beliefs and safeguard Christian faith in God.

In keeping with Melchior Mbonimpa, my work on faith-healing will pass through the "world in between,"[23] avoiding the fall either into kind of superstition that tries to manipulate God's supernatural powers; or into scientism, which pretends to know everything, including the unseen worlds. I want to apprehend a *world-in-between* to engage reason and faith, keeping humility of intelligence and engaging faith for understanding.

The methodology of this book makes use of a critical interdisciplinary approach. It provides an analysis based on theological and doctrinal developments, while using ethno-anthropological and bioethical approaches to lead us to a synthesis enlightened by Catholic bioethics.

Since issues related to faith-healing practices in Africa are too complex to cover, I will restrict my research to Sub-Saharan Africa, focusing specifically on the Great Lakes region of Africa which includes Rwanda and Burundi.

The book endeavors to contribute to the field of Catholic bioethics and the Church in Africa. I am indebted to the previous works of scholars which I have had a pleasure to read. These authors are Ludovic Lado, Stan Chu Ilo, Rosny Eric, Melchior Mbonimpa, Nestor Salumu Ndalibandu, Bernhard Udelhoven, Esther E. Acolatse, to name some of them. These scholars unveiled faith-healing ministry as an approach to healing of diseased Africans. Yet we need to foster understanding and pursue discernment regarding effective and ethical healing practices.

This book is an effort to respond to a dire need, inviting the Church and the society to keep a more critical eye on many people who devastated by suffering and diseases in Africa, to address the persistent failures in the medical care systems, and to refine the pastoral ministry to the sick. The book highlights the preferential option for the poor and compassion toward the needy, the sick and the broken; it calls upon a dialogue of faith and reason by engaging theological, social, and medical disciplines to discern on effective healing ministry. I hope this will equip us to act in view of the persistent failures in medical care and the popularity of faith-healing.

---

[23] Melchior Mbonimpa, *Guérison et Religion*, 6.

CHAPTER I

THE AFRICAN WORLDVIEW AND THE SEARCH FOR SPIRITUAL POWERS

In African Religion and Philosophy, John Mbiti writes,
Whatever science may do to prove the existence or non-existence of the spirits, one thing remains undeniable, namely that for African peoples the spirits are a reality and a reality which must be considered with whether it is clear, blurred or confused.[24] John Mbiti.

This first chapter describes the African religious worldview and highlights belief which Christian missionaries found on the continent. I consider the traditional religious belief as a remote substratum on which spiritual healing thrived in Africa. This calls for a renewal of Christian understanding of the spirit world to address illness and evil which continue to hamper the well-being and the flourishing of Africans.

Discerning the ministry of faith-healing in Africa calls for an examination of the African worldview and paying attention to belief in spiritual powers. It is important to have in mind that, as Esther E. Acolatse notes, the African search for supernatural powers is nothing bizarre in world Christianity, including Western Christianity. Far from being an African peculiarity, the search for spiritual healing powers and the fear of demonic forces and evil possession is a universal phenomenon. She writes,

> At the same time, people often ignore the fact that the history of Christianity in America is filled with experiences of the Spirit and belief in the powers as personal beings; in our day we can observe this fascination with evil at an unredeemable level, in literature, movies, and other media….neither the extreme dualism…that is the Christian South (notably Africa, and, to some extent, Latin America), nor the lackadaisical monism of…the North, bode well for exploring and understanding Christian belief and life according to the Spirit.[25]

---

[24] John Mbiti, *African Religion and Philosophy* (Oxford: Heinemann, 1990), 29.
[25] Esther E. Acolatse, *Powers, Principalities and the Spirit: Biblical Realism in Africa and the West* (Grand Rapids, MI: Eerdmans, 2018), 7.

In recent years, the South and the North have seen an emergence of religions of healing, as maintains the sociologist Regis Dericquebourg.[26] He refers to Georges Roux (1903-1981) in France, who was nicknamed the Christ of Montfavet. Roux based his teachings on the existence of the devil and on miraculous healings of illnesses and infirmities. Roux is universally known as the founder of the Universal Christian Church with disciples in many countries such as Belgium, United States, Germany, Switzerland, Italy, Gabon, and the Democratic Republic of Congo.

Catholic Christianity does not believe in the Christ of Montfavet, but in the resurrected Christ of Nazareth. As Pope Benedict wrote: "The Christian faith stands or falls with the truth and testimony that Christ is risen from the dead."[27] Harvey Cox maintains that the great spiritual traditions of humanity, both Europeans and Americans, despite the decline of the influence of religious institutions, did not renounce the divine spiritual powers during a rising secular society. In his words

> Europeans and Americans differ from each other about the secular, and the appropriate relationship between, religion, culture, and politics. But both are discovering that their assumptions about the role of religion in modern society place them in a distinct minority in a world that is also becoming modern, but that remains persistently religious. ... I do not believe this new interest is due to 'resacralization' that some observers speak of. It is due rather to the fact that certain deep-seated impulses have never died. They had once remained under the radar, out of sight of cultural elites, but they are now becoming more assertive and visible.[28]

Secularization which followed the era of the enlightenment and the industrial revolution have encouraged religious freedom and tolerance which are positive values, and these affect many religions and minority Catholic communities or threaten to be so. Pope John Paul calls for avoiding such a drama which accompanies secularization, the drama manifested by separation of faith and reason, which keeps God in suspense, and pretends to explain the universe as a

---

[26] Dericqueboug as cited in Melchior Mbonimpa, *Guérison et Religion en Afrique* (Paris: Harmattan, 2012), 8.

[27] I refer to the book of Joseph Ratzinger, Pope Benedict XVI, *Jesus of Nazareth* (London—Berlin: Bloomsbury, 2007), 320.

[28] Harvey Cox, *The Secular City* (Princeton, N. J: Princeton University Press 1965), xv. Harvey Cox illustrates today's religious phenomenon by exploring the rise of Pentecostal movements in various parts of the world in his recent book, *Fire from Heaven*. London: Cassel, 1996.

mere product of science. [29] The Pope challenges evils and ideologies associated with secularization, such as indifference, nihilism and agnosticism.[30]

As I look at the Global South, the number of churches, the increase of pastors and priests who are believed to perform healing miracles, is significant. Healing miracles as a crucial dimension of the prosperity gospel are indeed a chief drive of the phenomenal growth of Christianity in Africa as many scholars have argued.[31]

The Center of the Study of Global Christianity reveals that in 1910, only 9% of Africa's population was Christians, and 80% lived in just four countries: Ethiopia, South Africa, Egypt, and Madagascar. By 1970 Africa's Christian percentage had risen to 38.7%. Many were converts from ethno-religions in Sub-Saharan Africa. In 2010 Christian percentage was 48.3% and by 2020, it is expected to reach 49.3%. Roman Catholics form the largest block of Christian in Africa. Between 1970 and 2010 their numbers increased from 44.9 million (12.2% of the population) to 197 million (17.3%). In 2010 the Catholic share of the church members (34.2%) was lower than in 1970 (38. 3%). Projections for 2020 show an increase to 35.2%.[32]

The region of middle-Africa counted 30,113,000 Christians (73% of the population) in 1970. They rose to 134,618,000 Christians in 2020, representing 83% of the population.[33] Rwanda which had 2,292,000 Christians (61% of the population), will have 12, 042,000 (92% of the population) in 2020.[34] Such a growth of Christianity in Africa is indubitably good news. Yet such progress would be ephemeral if it did not bring up a profound and integral message of healing and liberation taught by Christ, to liberate each African and all Africans. The Post-Synodal Apostolic Exhortation *Africae Munus* puts it soundly,

> By accepting Jesus, Africa can receive incomparably effective and deep healing. Echoing the apostle Peter in the Acts of the Apostles (3:6), I

---

[29] Pope John Paul II, *Encyclical Letter Fides et Ratio: On The Relationship between Faith and Reason* (Libreria Editrice Vaticana,1998), 45.
[30] Ibid., 46
[31] S. D. Edwards et al, *Afro-Christian Religion and Healing in Southern Africa* (Lewiston—Lampeter: Edwin Mellen, 1988), 5.
[32] Ibid.
[33] https://www.gordonconwell.edu/ockenga/research/documents/2ChristianityinitsGlobalContext.pdf. Accessed on January 19, 2019.
[34] Ibid.

repeat: what Africa needs most is neither Gold nor Silver; she wants to stand up, like the man at the pool of Bethzatha; she wants to have confidence in herself and in her dignity as a people loved by her God. It is this encounter with Jesus which the Church must offer to bruised and wounded hearts yearning for reconciliation and peace, and craving for justice. We must provide and proclaim the word of Christ which heals, sets free and reconciles.[35]

The bishops call for a profound and integral healing of the whole of Africa and of each African. They see Africa, with its wounds from wars, diseases, insecurities, colonization, corruption, exploitation, fratricidal and tribal guerillas, and poverty, among many evils, as the person at the pool of Bethzatha searching for healing. We thus need to consider the problem of faith-healing as deeply social and theological. We need to go deeper into the African context on our path of discerning the question of faith-healing in the so-called cradle of humanity.

Unlike the scientific Western view which minimizes or pays no attention to the existence of spiritual powers, Christianity neither shares the African understanding of the world spirit nor denies the influence of malevolent of beneficent spirits. This needs however a more profound elaboration. In many instances in his teaching to the early church, as we read in Romans 6: 10-12 and in Ephesians 6:12, the apostle Paul did not lack to call upon believers to beware of their fight against spiritual forces, a battle whose terrible enemies are death and sin.[36] The Christian battle in Pauline letters is "not against flesh and blood, but against the rulers, against the authorities, against the powers of this dark world, and against the spiritual forces in heavenly realms." (Rom 6:10-12). Yet for Christians, spiritual forces should not be feared, they are in the words of Karl Bath, "lordless lords" and "powers, abilities and possibilities of life."[37] Spiritual forces are not taken as entities *per se,* but in the words of Esther Acolatse, "spirits behind human's fierce independence and not in any way suggestive of otherworldly created beings."[38] Thus, as Baxter's *Practical Works,* and his section "Unpardonable Sins Against the Holy Spirit" maintain,

---

[35] See the Post-Synodal Apostolic Exhortation, *Africae Munus* http://w2.vatican.va/content/benedict-xvi/en/apost_exhortations/documents/hf_ben-xvi_exh_20111119_africae-munus.html#III.The_world_of_health_care. Accessed on January 19, 2019.

[36] Esther Acolatse, *Powers, Principalities, and the Spirit* (Grand Rapids, MI, Eerdmans, 2018),

[37] Karl Bath as cited by Esther Acolatse, *Powers, Principalities and the Spirit*, 190.

[38] Ibid.

It would be pointless to get into any kind of argument with people about whether the Evil One exists or not, since it would be nonsense to attribute to the Devil the source and power of the miracles of Jesus if he were not believed to exist and be real, as the Jewish authorities did.[39]

My contention of spiritual powers does not intend to call back Africans to some inadequate ancient traditions, to promote popular spiritualism deprived of human accountability in doing good and evil. A deeper discernment is required within faith and reason.

Christ has conquered the Evil One and Christians are the heirs of His Spirit sent as a message of compassion to the poor, the Word that heals the sick and brokenhearted persons, upholds the freedom of the oppressed, and the recovery of the sight for the blind (Lk 4:18). The message brought by Christ to African believers can effectively bring them the healing that they thirst for from ancient times. As Laurenti Magesa observes, the essence of Christ's message can effectively meet the African *ethos* that seeks, cares for, and aspires for "an abundant life."[40]

To go on with, this first chapter guides us into sub-Saharan Africa, with a focus on the Great Lakes region of central Africa. I (1) describe major features of this African worldview and (2) illustrate it by using the *Ryangombe* and *Kubandwa* cults of *Banyarwanda* of Ruanda (approximately those living in Rwanda of today). (3) I underline miraculous healings and exorcisms within Christianity as a way of witnessing to Christ's compassion for the poor, the outcast and care for sick persons, thus a call to Africans today. (4) Based on the early Christian narratives, especially on the Pauline Letters, I highlight a need for a realistic approach that considers prayer as a possibility for healing and medicine as a curative remedy.

This book has both a subjective and objective motivation. The Great Lakes region of Africa, particularly Rwanda, is the very area in which I have been brought up. Thus, I have some personal understanding of the complexities surrounding healing and the spirit world. As Mbonimpa says, "In Africa more than elsewhere, the correlation of healing and religion has reached its

---

[39] See Richard Baxter's *Practical Works* as cited by E. Acolatse, *Powers, Principalities and The Spirit* (Grand Rapids, MI: William B. Eerdmans, 2018), 191.

[40] Fr. Laurenti Magesa is a Catholic diocesan priest and currently a professor of theology at Hekima University College, in Nairobi, Kenya. He has tremendously published in the field of African religion and spirituality. Magesa argues that African religion derives from God, and the basis of its morality is no other than promotion of life. Laurenti Magesa, *African Religion: The Moral Traditions of Abundant Life*. New York: Orbis, 1997.

paroxysmal point.⁴¹ Mbonimpa's consideration is experienced through daily conversations with people where the power of God is constantly referred to as the ultimate solution to whatever matters, especially health and wealth. One's success or achievement is for many Africans a sign of God's blessing. The contrary is interpreted as mischance brought by the Devil. As one goes back to Africa after spending a time in the West, he/she will notice a God-imbued lexicon and be impressed by seeing burgeoning churches in the urban and rural areas. He/she would hear common messages such as "God is in control" or "Christ is the answer", just "Pray in the name of Jesus." That ubiquitous and strong African religiosity is noted by Paul Kagame, the current president of Rwanda, during the 2019 National Prayer Breakfast.

> I do not think there is any place in the world which would be more prayerful than Africa…but we should pair our prayers with works…praying should not only be a matter of praising and interceding, but prayer should also bring us power to do what we are assigned to do, and this should be visible by its fruits.⁴²

The mushrooming of Christian churches and the increase in religiosity is statistically viewed by Caleb O. Oladipo in *Wealth, Health, and Hope in African Christian Religion*. The author observes a unique growth of the Christian churches and affirms: "Black African societies can no longer be conceived apart from Christian experience."⁴³ The same author shows that in 1900 there were 8,756,000 Christians in Africa, which represents approximatively 1.6 % of the global Christian population. In 2005, African Christians were 389,304,000 (18.5 % Christians worldwide). The growth is as highest as 4,000 % in the twentieth century with an annual growth of 2.5 %.⁴⁴

The growth of African Christianity has to do with the search for healing powers. In Rwanda and Burundi as in many sub-Saharan countries, belief in supernatural powers does not require sophisticated instruments to discern, it just "sticks out a mile" as Mbonimpa would say.⁴⁵ Across the world, Christian and

---

[41] Melchior Mbonimpa, *Guérison et Religion*, 9.
[42] Kagame Paul, as cited in https://www.newtimes.co.rw/timestv/national-prayer-breakfast-speech-president-kagame. Accessed on January 14, 2019.
[43] Caleb O. Olapido "African Christianity, its Scope in Global Context" in *Wealth, Health and Hope in African Christian Religion*. ed. Stan Chu Ilo (Lanham—London: Lexington, 2018), 5.
[44] Ibid.
[45] Mbonimpa, *Guérison et Religion*, 9.

traditional healers abound, either using prayers or natural remedies such as herbs, or combining both. There are seers, diviners, prophets and prophetesses, astrologists, people who are believed to possess mysterious powers to predict natural events or heal mental, and physical ailments.[46] Belief in the existence of the spirit world is tied to the search for health and wealth, as it is in the case of Abrahamic religions, with Christianity and Islam which are now predominant in Africa. Spiritual powers are part of religious practices and belief in the religions. But the question needs to be addressed: is the traditional African understanding compatible with Christianity and Christian practices? This is the key question behind this research.

1.1. An African Worldview and Spiritual Healing

From an African worldview, Sylvestre Bancira, a Burundian scholar, divides the African primal universe into three principal realms: (1) the material world, sensible, visible *microcosmos*, (2) the intermediary world of spirits and all sorts of benevolent and malevolent spirits (*mesocosmos*), and (3) the supra-sensible world of great heroes, mythical beings, and the divine realm.[47] It is believed that illness and healing are the result of the interaction and relationship between the *microcosmos* and the *mesocosmos*.[48] Gabiro wa Gatumu states that " most African see supernatural powers as hierarchical structure. This structure is explained by Bancira Sylvestre.

> The lowest structure includes lifeless creation at the base, next the animate non-human creation and then human beings. This lower structure is the arena where supernatural powers exercise their influence. Ancestral spirits are closer to people. They are the link between the lowest and highest structures and occupy the middle structure. The higher structure consists of spirits who are slightly above the ancestors but lower than God who takes the highest position. ...it is God who allows the spirits to supervise the everyday affairs of humankind. The spirits manifest God's power, wrath and other attributes as his messenger and agents. They personify God in nature, in the earth, cultivable land, forests, mountains, rocks, rivers, seas, and lakes in weather, air, wind and hailstorm. [49]

---

[46] Bancira Sylvestre as cited by Mbonimpa, *Guérison et Religion*, 9.
[47] Bancira Sylvestre cited in *Guérison et Religion en Afrique...* 58.
[48] Mbonimpa, *Guérison et Religion*, 58.
[49] Kabiro wa Gatumu, *The Pauline Concept of Supernatural Powers*. A Reading from African Worldview (Eugene, OR: Wipf & Stock, 2008), 61.

The African worldview places the supreme being, God, in the highest category. God is believed to be the source of all powers, and nothing goes beyond God. The ancestral spirits are accessible, they can expedite or inhibit human existence. Spirit power is sought for human success, guidance and directing the universe. People are thus required to maintain good relationship with spirits. Africans believe that the latter can materialize in the real world in the form of animals, old people, babies, birds; thus, people should pay much attention since no one knows in which forms the spirits will visit them! They are at the same time respected and feared. Such perception and fear of power of spirits would have no room in Christianity where Christ holds the supreme power. "All authority has been given to me in heaven and on earth" (Mt 28:18). African Traditional Religion does not know the power of Christ.

There is a distinctive aspect between the African and Western worldview. This has been a contributing factor to problems western missionaries encountered in evangelizing Africa, and difficulties medical missionaries met in providing modern medicine to Africans. As Kabiro wa Gatumu highlights,

> the Africans perceived reality through a lens produced by the African primal worldview, which typically grants supernatural powers real existence. Most Africans not only agree to the existence of supernatural powers but also allow them to influence human existence. They have always given supernatural powers a phobic allegiance, which persists despite the rapid growth of Christianity and the frequent use of the Bible.[50]

The author observes that Africans "recognize powerful spirits that are not human, residing in the spirit world but naturally permeate the physical world, making it possible for the spirit world and the material world to intersect, to interact and network dynamically."[51] Many scholars such as John Mbiti agree with these strong beliefs in the spirit world in Africa.

John Mbiti dedicated a study to three hundred different peoples of the continent. He accounts the presence of a "myriad of spirits" in all African societies. Mbiti's conclusion is provocative: "Whatever science may do to prove the existence or non-existence of the spirits, one thing remains undeniable,

---

[50] Kabiro wa Gatumu, *The Pauline Concepts of Supernatural Powers: A Reading from African Worldview* (Eugene, OR: Wipf and Stock, 2008), 25.
[51] Kabiro wa Gatumu, *The Pauline Concepts of Supernatural Powers*, 6.

namely that for African peoples the spirits are a reality and a reality which must be considered with whether it is clear, blurred or confused."[52]

The African worldview was neither welcomed by missionaries nor is it fully shared by all Africans in todays' era of scientific discoveries. Yet as many African and Western researchers in social sciences and religion have noted, most Africans, both educated and uneducated think the realness and actuality of spiritual powers.[53] Christian missionaries opposed the primal African view of the spirit world, yet a considerable number of Africans who espoused Christian faith did not fully hold the worldview of their evangelizers. They have stayed, as the former archbishop of Zambia, Emmanuel Milingo states: "in the world in between"[54] the Christian faith and the world of African tradition. What follows highlights major features of the African worldview.

The first feature of the African worldview is *the association of the sacred and the profane*. African societies are not generally secular. The spiritual world and the material world constitute two sides of the same coin. A traditional African view conceives the reality by spiritual means. What occurs to a person or to his/ her milieu is easily attached to an influence of spirits? The African worldview sees that "alien supernatural forces stand behind whatever happens to humankind in history and in their structure of existence."[55] In ancient Rwanda, an unknown wild beast, which introduces itself in a region and kills people, was allegedly seen as spirit-possessed or a divine envoy. Similar examples are found across African traditional cultures. Among the Gikuyu of Kenya, when a carnivorous animal eats sacrificial meat, it was interpreted those spirits have accepted the sacrifice and so sent one of them in the form of animal to consume the sacrifice. In West Africa, when a domestic animal behaves strangely, it must be killed and buried to chase away the evil spirit riding on it.[56] These examples apply to natural disasters, to health and sickness. It is believed that the spirits

---

[52] John Mbiti as cited in Robert E. *Moses, Practices of Power* (Indiana: MN: Fortress Press, 2014), 219.

[53] Kabiro wa Gatumu, *The Pauline Concepts of Supernatural Powers*, 25. See also Bernhard Udelhoven, *Unseen Worlds*. Spirits, Witchcraft, and Satanism. Lusaka, FENZA Publications, 2015), 65.

[54] Emmanuel Milingo, a former Archibishop of Zambia (1960-1983) is known to have been at the fore front of healing and exorcism in African Catholic Christianity. However, his so-claimed gift of healing was perceived by Vatican as unbiblical and disastrous to the administration of the Zambian Church. In 1983, Milingo was resigned from his episcopate and with his undoctrinal positions, the former prelate was excommunicated in 2006. Milingo healing ministry is echoed in many books including, *The World in Between,* Maryknoll, N.Y: Orbis, 1984.

[55] Ibid.

[56] L. S. B. Leakey as cited by Kabiro wa Gatumu, *The Pauline Concepts of Supernatural Powers*, 45.

infuse an animal, a person, or any entity associated with the misfortune or the sickness they cause.

That which is understood as spirit calls our attention here. Spirit was seen as "a personal entity but without a material body,"[57] as "shadows which exist within or without the material reality."[58] Some scholars think of existence of spirits, but the latter are always conceivable as taking forms of concrete things, such as birds, animals or natural sites.[59] For Samuel G. Kibicho, belief in spirits is the reason why, in order to avoid contamination from diseases or any harm, restrictions and taboos are to be observed toward sanctified animals and objects which embody spirits.[60]

Not only an individual animal or an object is believed to be a domain of a spirit but also the universe is a dwelling of spiritual powers. The African primal view would enjoy hearing the Psalm of creation (Ps. 19) which praises the world as a manifestation of God, the divine mighty power and munificence. As R.H. Codrington asserts, the African world view contemplates the universe and its natural features as a living reality, with its personality, with will and life forces.[61] African traditional religion conceives the world as a divine *oeuvre*. The respect, reverence, and awe which is given to material world is for Africans a moral obligation since the world is a *theophanaeia*, a manifestation of God's power and benevolence. Thus, in the African primal view, the rites and rituals have less to praise or respect a place or a temple than to revere the supernatural power of the divine which dwells in it. The role of this feature could be validated by the fact that God supports and protects the life of individual creations and helps human sustenance by the spirits.

The second feature of the African worldview is *the attribution of unknown or unfamiliar events to new spirits*. This fits in with what Mircea Eliade wrote in *Patterns in Comparative Religions:* "everything unusual, unique, new, perfect, or monstrous at once becomes imbued with *magico-religious* power and an object of veneration or fear according to the circumstances."[62] Education brought by the West was something unusual to indigenous Africans. Africans

---

[57] Ibid.

[58] Ibid.

[59] See John Mbiti, *New Testament Eschatology in an African Background* (London Univesity Press, 1971), 137. See also Bolaji E. Idowu, *African Traditional Religion* (Maryknoll, N.Y: Orbis, 1975), 4.

[60] Samuel Kibicho, "The Continuity of the African Conception of God into and through Christianity", 372.

[61] Robert. H. Codrington, *The Melanesians Studies in Their Anthropology and Folklore* (Oxford: Clarendon Press, 2012), 119.

[62] See Mircea Eliade cited in *Guérison et Religion...* 46.

were taught alphabets, they learned how to write, to speak, to produce a paper, and publish a book. This was considered at first glance as a Western spirit (*ikizungu*). From an oral culture in communication, Africans were introduced to writing letters instead of sending a vocal messenger. Culture dies hard, but it can. There has been reluctance to learn from a Western culture which was seen as an alien spirit, with suspicion that written record is a means to control everyone. There has been some hesitancy among Africans to save money in banks when Africans saved money in pottery or in cows' horns. One could find this view as a process of learning and discernment. Despite this, the so-called western spirit brought new things, and found Africans imbued with a faculty to learn, to acquire new experiences and to develop a new understanding.

This suggests that the African worldview is not fixed; it is dynamic, it can accommodate a new understanding of spirit and powers "that ease life and get rid of occult supernatural powers, which may prove ineffectual."[63] As Kabiro wa Gatumu asserts, western education has had an influence on the number of spirits in African religion, both by increasing them and decreasing them. Yet, in the view of Kwame Bediako and John Mbiti, while divinities can be acquired or dropped when they become useless, ancestral spirits remain irreplaceable.[64]

The third feature of the African religious world view is the way in which *social status is interpreted through a spiritual lens*. Priesthood, leadership, and kingship have been traditionally associated with spiritual powers. The African traditional mindset sees priests, and kings as "special agents and representative in ruling people."[65] Thus a good governor who promotes the welfare and warfare of a nation is seen as a recipient of benevolent spirits, he/she deserves respect and honor. On the contrary, a bad king or ruler who undermines the welfare and warfare of a community, with calamities, disasters, and insecurity falling on the citizens, would be considered as an emissary of malevolent spirits; he would not deserve respect and honor. But such an observation could be problematic. The Sub-Saharan communities are most of the time tribally oriented. The criteria of welfare could be tribally motivated. One tribe could be enjoying good life to the detriment of another.[66] African religion considers

---

[63] Kabiro wa Gatumu, *The Pauline Concept of Supernatural Powers,* 47.

[64] See Kwame Bediako, *Jesus in Africa: The Christian Gospel in African History and Experience* (Akropong-Akuapem, Ghana: Regnum Africa, 2000), 90., John Mbiti, *African Religions* (London: Oxford University Press, 1971), 77.

[65] John Mbiti, *The Concept of God in Africa* (London: SPCK, 1970), 122.

[66] What happened to Rwanda in 1959 and in 1994 questions many researchers. The regime ruled in favor of one tribal group called Hutu. Tutsi were taken into exile and discriminated in many spheres of national politics. Conflict amid the Rwandan population became even the worst horror of the twentieth century: The genocide perpetrated against Tutsi

benevolent spirits as familiar while malevolent spirits are alien. This gives a hint as to why some African societies are marked by tribal wars. There is a tendency to interpret politics, economy, and health in spiritual terms. It is widely known that African royal families, and their subjects both consulted benevolent spirits, hoping to get through them to the supreme being.[67]

The fourth feature is *the recognition of human ability to control spirits, except the Supreme being*. There are people in the African communities who are believed to have special powers of bringing down spirits or driving them away. Suffering or illness is associated with evil people, the witches. Some people are afraid to cause evil through uttering cruel words, having evil intentions, or engaging in wrong deeds. An evil person incarnates evil spirits when he/she can suppress flourishing life and obstruct vital energies. Witches are also associated with misfortunes, disharmony, and insecurity. A person who is suspected of harboring evil spirits is isolated and even killed to preserve others from contamination.

This is a clear case of the violation of human rights, and it is against African ethics. These killings are not remote facts when Reuters recently reported about thousands of elderly Tanzanians who have been killed for being witches.[68] Every person needs peace, harmony, health and wealth, and these derive from good spirits in the African worldview. In case of the contrary, something or someone must bear the responsibility. In the African tradition, the aim is thus to preserve the welfare of the society between the living and the dead, the born and the not-yet born, the harmony between the world spirit and material world, which is pursued through performing rites and rituals.[69]

The description of the African worldview should not be taken as an adequate basis for contemporary ethics, but to the largest extent as metaphor. The modern political, religious and socio-economic context does not support the fact of attributing all that happens to spiritual world. Human responsibility must be accounted for. "Failing to see human responsibility in incidents that are hostile to human life is as good as abusing the African worldview, which hold the spirits act according to human conduct."[70] A government which does not provide vaccination to its people and finds children dying of tetanus, measles

---

in 1994. The president of the time was highly praised as a father of the nation, despite injustices and inequalities. Rwanda is today on an arduous path of reconciliation. It stays a long way to heal memories and attain to a reconciled nation.

[67] Kabiro wa Gatumu, *The Pauline Concept of Supernatural Powers*, 48.

[68] See http://www.africanews.com/2017/08/01/tanzania-witch-killings-claimed-479-lives-from-january-june-2017-report// accessed on January 19, 2019.

[69] Kabiro wa Gatumu, *The Pauline Concept of Supernatural Powers*, 48.

[70] Ibid.

and tuberculosis should be accounted for. A bad spirit may be the lack of health policy to protect a nation from epidemics. A ministry of public transport which does not provide adequate roads for vehicles and pedestrians should not blame bad spirits for possessing drivers when accidents occur. A traffic police which does not rigorously provide road signs and instruct the public about traffic rules should not impute road accidents to unknown spirits. Although education, legislation, and responsibility do not imply that everything will become perfection, and so there would no longer be diseases or accidents; imputing everything to supernatural powers, without confronting the social causes of illnesses, could even make things much worse and escalate the rate of morbidity and mortality in the sub-Saharan Africa. After sketching key elements of African worldview, we need to examine the African traditional religion by focusing more on traditional healers.

1.2. AFRICAN TRADITIONAL RELIGION (ATR) AND HEALERS

The section above emphasized some characteristics of the African worldview and shed light on the African primal belief and its dark side in today's Africa. In search for an ethical approach to healing, analysis of healers in African religion is required. Healers in sub-Saharan Africa call our attention as they represent a place of active compassion toward the sick, the care for the impoverished and crucified people of sub-Saharan Africa. They are people who, despite being rich in natural resources, of spirituality and religion, has been exploited, enslaved and uncared for. Although African traditional healing could be to some extent seen as a mythological and less developed in view of modern medicine, considering spiritual healers meets a Christian call to stand together, to accompany and to be compassionate in caring for our brothers and sisters crushed by evils, including illnesses and diseases. Philips Brigs and Janice Booth refer to the cult of Lyangombe in their exploration of ancient and contemporary Rwanda: "the cult of Lyangombe became an important force of social cohesion" amidst Rwandan tribal tensions, "Lyangombe is propitiated by *Imandwa, a* political religious fraternity who performs rituals, chants, and dances in his honor."[71] The religion was responding to a social tension and anxiety perpetrated by inequity and poverty perpetrated by the monarchical system and which German-Belgian colonial regime rendered even worse.

Many researchers of the Great Lakes, especially of Rwanda, relate the search of Lyangombe religion for fighting against poverty which was ravaging

---

[71] Philip Briggs, *Bradt Travel Guide*, 6th ed. (England: IDC House, 2016), 27.

the nation. The *Borgen Project* shows that during the time of the monarchs (1500-1900), and in the time of German colonial rule (1889-1910), as well as in the time of Belgian colonial rule (1916-1962) Rwandans were torn apart by ethnic conflicts. The country was ravaged by misery after World War I due loss of valuable land to neighboring countries. The mass of people was desperately poor.[72] The majority of peasants was subjugated by the monarchs. Still, as Gary B. Ferngreen notes, in the nineteenth century, European colonial powers, Germans and Belgians in our case, "were not initially interested in providing medical services to the general populations of colonial possessions."[73] Colonialists maintained the monarchical and unequal system, and the natural resources which were to help in addressing health *status quo* were sent in their country of origin. As many researchers attest, colonialists even rendered the situation worse by empowering and vindicating the system through education and in spreading a divisive ideology through the whole territory.

A Rwandan proverb says: One who is trapped inside a house caught on fire must find all means for rescue (*uhiriye mu nzu ntaho adapfunda imitwe*). In case of ill-health such as infertility, Malaria, physical wounds, mental problems and what is called evil possession, the available remedy was provided by traditional-spiritual healers. Traditional and spiritual healing was highly tied to beliefs in benevolent spirits which put into herbs healing principles, and that God can empower the healers. Traditional-spiritual healing was all-encompassing, including cure and prevention of evil spirits, the search for the safe delivery of a baby, good weather and land prosperity. This search was promoted in the cult known as *Kubandwa* or consecration to the spirits.

As Nothomb observes, the cult of *Kubandwa* became successful due to "a persistent anxiety caused by the rigidity of the entire social structure and the pessimism of religious thought among all Hutus and many Tutsi."[74] What happened in ancient Rwanda echoes what was going on in Burundi.

Sylvestre Bancira's work "Possession among *Baganza* Spirits and Healing Rituals of *Kubandwa* in Burundi,"[75] sheds light on indigenous healing practices in Burundi. According to Bancira, evil possession should not be

---

[72] The Brogen Project. https://borgenproject.org/causes-of-poverty-in-rwanda. Accessed on February 18, 2019.

[73] Ferngren B. Gary, *Medicine and Religion* (Baltimore: MD, 2014), 169.

[74] Heusch cited by Simon Bizimana, *Le Culte de Ryangombe au Rwanda* (Tervuren: Belgique, Musee Royal d'Afrique Centrale, 2018), 58.

[75] In reference to the book of Sylvestre Bancira, *Possession par les Esprits Baganza et Rituels du Thérapeutique du Kubandwa au Burundi* (Bujumbura, Université du Burundi, 1990).

mythologized, it exists and it can be described as any other illness. Bancira provides a series of manifestations of evil possession: These includes refusal to eat, stubborn behavior, unsettledness, hiccough, seeking out deserted places like in marshes, water waterfalls, dense forests, or on mountain tops, where one might think there are evil spirits.[76] Mgr. Tournyol du Clos, in his book, *The Advanced Battle of the Church: A Practical Approach of Exorcism*,[77] provides a detailed symptomatology of evil possession. On the spiritual level, an evil-possessed patient in need of exorcism is characterized by pride, revolt and revulsion, blasphemy against faith, doubt toward the sacred, occultism, opposition against prayers, refusal of the love of God, despair, etc. On physical level, the patient is characterized by spasms, tetany, epilepsy, hysteria. The person affected by evil spirits may complain from headache, stomachache or suffers from spinal pain. [78]

Yet in the view of Mbonimpa, the symptoms of evil spirit possession should not be taken as a rule. Most of the time there is combat between an evil spirit and the patient, and to recognize spirit possession, a medium or a clairvoyant must be consulted. The latter is believed to be possessed by spirits which confer on him/her power and competence.

One does not decide to consult the medium alone. Family members or relatives of the patient must be consulted since healing engages the whole community. The society takes seriously what the spirit medium says and roughly knows the difference between spirit possession and psychopathological ailments. Trances which characterize a patient are not to be taken as a psychopathological issue. Bancira wrote:

> Rather than an individualistic psychopathology that seeks mental sickness or madness in the personality of the patient and interferes with his personal life story, the traditional conception seeks to name the unknown, and therefore what matters are forces that animate the person in social relationships. To say to the patient: 'these are spirits which possess 'reassures him/her and opens to him an area of unsuspected behavior recognized in his/her group. To say to him/her:' it is your mind or your imagination which is sick' would be nonsense and would precipitate madness in the subject since it would have no other choice than to conceive him/herself as the only one of that kind, a monster cut off from the common sense and from the community. By the same token, the

---

[76] Ibid., 38.

[77] I have translated the title in English, and the original copy is in French. See Mgr Tournyol du Clos. *Le Combat Avancé de l'Eglise*, (Beyrouth: Architratège, 2004), 138.

[78] Ibid., 139.

patient would lose his/her identity, given that personality in a traditional environment cannot be conceived apart from belonging to the family group and the clan.[79]

The consulted medium may provide different herbal sedative preparations. In this case, she/he acts at the same time as a diviner and a healer. He/She could also refer the patient to any healer or prescribe an initiation to divination. The patient reaches a desirable status. This at a certain extent explains the higher number of women who get involved in the world of spirit possession in Africa, as Bancira asserts:

> Female diviners generally emancipate themselves from the rules and constraints governing women in traditional settings. They can especially sit and drink with men, hold the palaver and even unthinkable privilege- choose their husband; possession by the spirits can lead to a true liberation of the subject that is affected and especially if it is a woman.[80]

The diviner can finally prescribe an initiation to the cult of Ryangombe which is the highest healing remedy above all resources and envisaged advantages. Few people could afford the healing by Lyangombe. The following paragraphs help us understand the healing religion of Lyangombe in the ancient Great Lakes Region of Africa.

1.3. Lyangombe as a Healer among Banyarwanda

Not everyone who is possessed could be healed by Lyangombe. Scholars describe four stages to reach Lyangombe healing. (1) One must be proven under the attack of evil spirits and become grievously sick. (2) The person must have consulted a medium for the prescription after a diagnosis. A medium provides a prescription when the spirits have identified themselves through the mouth of the patient. (3) The patient must have undergone some rites and rituals or taken prescriptions provided by the healer who is not necessarily the one who consulted with him. (4) The healing must be effective before an initiation into the society of Lyangombe.[81]

The initiation to Lyangombe has a twofold role. First, it seeks to prevent relapse into evil possession. Second, it is an occasion of thanksgiving to be healed and saved by Lyangombe. The initiation consists in vowing to be

---

[79] Syvestre Bancira, *Possession par les Esprits: Baganza et Rituel Thérapeutique du Kubandwa au Burundi* (Berlin:Verlag Nicht Ermitterlbar,1990), 38-39.

[80] Sylvestre Bancira, *Possession par les Esprits Baganza*, 45.

[81] Melchior Mbonimpa, *Guérison et Religion*, 60.

possessed by Lyangombe, to be indwelt by him and espoused by him, whether one is male or female. Far from being a malevolent spirit, Lyangombe is believed to be a benevolent spirit, a spirit of happiness as Luc de Heusch expresses it.[82]

Vincent Mulago gwa Cikala Musharamina is a Catholic priest from the Democratic Republic of Congo (D.R.C-Congo). He is known as a father of Bantu philosophy and a pillar of African theology. He is also a founder of the Center of African Religions. He published vastly in the field of African traditional religion of the Bantu people and their worldview.[83] He is a Catholic theologian who witnessed the half of the twentieth century in Africa, at the juncture of Christianity and African tradition. His works shed light on the way in which initiation is performed for a person who enters the society of Lyangombe.

For Mulago, the initiation introduces the follower into an invisible society of the faithful of Lyangombe on earth, and later, into a celestial kingdom where Lyangombe is surrounded by 30 ministers, among his elect. The society does not have a hierarchical structure; it rather knows ritual celebrations where Lyangombe the supreme leader is represented in the person of his principal minister. The celebrating minister is always the same one. According to Mulago, the society of Lyangombe knows two levels: the first that moves a layperson to be an initiate, and the second that moves the initiate to be an elect. The latter means that one shares the seat of Lyangombe. At this third level, one obtains the plenitude of priesthood while on the second, one has the honor to officiate at rituals.[84] Scholars present diverging views as regards the life of Lyangombe. The works of Dominic Nothomb, a Catholic priest of the Society of Missionaries of Africa (White Fathers), sought to understand the meaning of rites and stories in the belief in Lyangombe. For Nothomb, Lyangombe may have lived under the reign of Ruganzu II Ndoli (1467-1500), and there would have been clashes between men who claimed the same title of King (although Lyangombe's kingship was of a spiritual nature). This implies that the cult of Lyangombe would have spread in various kingdoms of the region from Rwanda, even if there is no evidence that the hero himself is a Rwandan by birth.

---

[82] Luc de Heusch, as cited by Melchior Mbonimpa, *Guérison et Religion*, 60.

[83] See Mulago gwa Cikala. *La Religion Traditionelle des Bantu et Leur Vision du Monde* (Kinshassa: Faculté de Théologie Catholique,1980.

[84] Vincent Mulago, "Initiation Africaine et Initiation Chretienne" In *Lyangombe, Mythes et Rites. Actes du Deuxième Colloque du Ceruki* (Bukavu, Congo: Edition Ceruki, 1980), 29.

Lyangombe might have come from a neighboring kingdom. Under the monarch Mutara I Semugeshi (1500-1533) the cult of Lyangombe was opposed by the kings, but eventually he became respected and honored because of a plague which spread over the entire territory. Since the king owned many cows, the herd was decimated. The diviners of the time found the cause of the disaster in Lyangombe's blood that the kingdom (the land) had drunk. To repulse the evil, rituals must be performed and cultic offerings had to be rendered to Lyangombe.[85] The scholars do not specify the place of birth of Lyangombe and the itinerary of his adventures. What is recited are wars involving this hero along with monarchies in the Great Lakes region of Africa.

Lyangombe arose in a milieu where God (*Imana*) was understood as creator, eternal, righteous, powerful, transcendent, and invisible. This was a God such as described by Mircea Eliade in world religions and which, according to him, helps us understand the religious history of humanity as whole.[86] Since God is inaccessible, there is no cult, no song, no poem, no chant to offer to it.[87] But the Banyarwanda practiced some rituals in the divine honor and some of them today still practice rituals to ancestors. The latter are dead, but people believe that their physical powers, and their intellectual powers remain and operate in living people. It is believed that ancestors intervene positively or negatively in earthly events. They can heal sickness and they can cause illness. Thus, the ancestors require offerings and prayers to be favorable toward the living ones. Fear of a transcendent God and an attack of ancestor spirits is what motivate the cults to ancestors. This was a fundamental component of religious belief in the area where cults of Lyangombe prospered. It is within these cults and belief which were addressed to ancestors where the new cult to Lyangombe arose.

Simon Bizimana and Jean Baptiste Nkurikiyinka are both initiated to the cults of Lyangombe. In their book, *The Cults of Ryangombe in Rwanda,* the authors refer to the prayers addressed to Lyangombe. The prayer brings to light some of concrete problems the population of Rwanda was going through. They were yearning for prosperity, livelihood, property, for children in good health. Rooted in their traditional beliefs, people were beseeching God to protect them from female and male evil spirits (ancestor spirits). Below we find a typical prayer addressed by Lyangombe elect interceding for Lyangombe followers.

---

[85] Dominique Nothomb, "Signification Religieuse des Recits et des Rites de Lyangombe" In Lyangombe, *Mythes et Rites. Actes du Deuxième Colloque du Ceruki* (Bukavu: Ceruki, 1979), 110.

[86] See Mercia Eliade, *Chamanisme et les Technique de l'Extase* (Paris: Payot, 1968.

[87] Dominique Nothomb, "Signification Religieuse des Recits", 111.

> Be always with *Imana* (Lyangombe)
> Be prosperous
> Receive this offering that we present to you
> Be our victory
> Help us survive
> Give us property, grassy fields, and cows
> Help us to produce abundant crops
> Give us a safe delivery and children in good health
> Protect us from sorcerers, male ghosts, as well as female ones.[88]

As Nothomb states, in various accounts about Lyangombe, *Imana*, the Creator- God has no role to play while Lyangombe has much to do. However, Lyangombe was not divinized. He was understood as a man enjoying a great magic power, but with a lot of weaknesses, lacking skills and intelligence in the game, lying, letting himself be seduced, disobeying his mother, disgracing a girl, losing his possessions, and eventually getting killed while hunting.[89] The cults around Lyangombe gives hope of overcoming poverty, morbidity and mortality, and frustrations of life within a traditional religion marked by lack of hope, and domination of moral and systemic evils. Unlike the invisible God who seemed to have forgotten human beings, Lyangombe is with the people, he talks to them, people can address him prayers through his elect on earth, and he would respond to them. As Nothomb expresses, the cults of Lyangombe and *kubandwa* introduced a democratic religion which negates the division of the real society founded on the ownership of cattle… We do not accept the functional interpretation offered by Marquet, according to which Lyangombe cult would serve only as an additional factor of cohesion, uniting into a single belief system members of different castes…the ritual of the Lyangombe rested on the mystical and radical negation of the established order.[90]

Lyangombe as a clandestine society worked as a family full of promises in which the initiate was welcomed. Lyangombe therefore was giving his followers what they felt the Creator-God was not offering. People had belief that

---

[88] Simon Bizimana, Jean Baptiste Nkurikiyinka, *Le Culte de Ryangombe au Rwanda* (Tevuren Belgique: Musée Royal de l'Afrique Centrale, 2018), 61. Original in French. Accessed online February 18, 2019.
https://www.africamuseum.be/sites/default/files/media/docs/research/publications/rmca/online/documents-social-sciences-humanities/ryangombe.pdf. Accessed on February 18, 2019.
[89] Dominique Nothomb, *"Signification Religieuse des Recits"*, 107.
[90] Luc de Heusch, *Le Rwanda et La Civilisation Interlacustre* (Brussels : Institut de Sociologie, 1966), 172.

Lyangombe assists them in everyday life. Lyangombe filled the religious void caused by the absence of the distant God. He also developed around them a cult, a liturgy with sacred instruments, with ornaments, with gestures, with words, songs, declamation and dance, an African folklore which is seen by some scholars as a platform to express "pain and suffering, joy and sadness, love and thankfulness"[91] It was, in the view of Bancira Sylvestre, a healing ritual.

Lyangombe caused a shift in the traditional cult of ancestors, promoting a "communitarian belief in God" and solidaristic bonds in which African ethics thrived.[92] Before Lyangombism, the family ancestors were restricted to only a small circle of the family and their influence was often harmful, destructive, and deadly. Lyangombe and the members of his cult brought a new class of ancestors that do not attach to the living by the blood bonds. They could always intervene in a beneficial way, in favor of the new members from any family, from any clan, from any caste, and even from any nation.

On one hand, the relationship between family ancestors and the living is short-lived: family ancestors no longer act on their fourth-generation offspring. So, these family ancestors do not roam forever underground, they disappear after a while. On the other hand, Lyangombe is a great inventor of an after-life among the *Banyarwanda* and *Barundi*. He lives amid his elect, not in the underground and dreadful place where vanish our joys offered by earthily existence, but between heaven and earth, in a sort of paradise at the top of high mountains, the volcanoes of Kalisimbi and Muhabura in the northern Rwanda, where he hears his elect who enter after death into life that does not end. As their master, the disciples of Lyangombe believe they will become immortal citizens, enjoying the high top and calm highlands, which they consider as their heaven. Nothomb wrote:

> They are not only existing ones after death. They are alive. They drink, they smoke, they hunt. They are therefore happy…they appear in men who reproduce their deeds. For centuries already, and without discrimination of races, origin, of sex, social status, they lead a human happy life.[93]

The attainment of blessedness and happiness in life in Lyangombe cults is not a function of virtue or merit. It is not conquered by power or struggle. It results

---

[91] Bénézet Bujo, Foundations of An African Ethic (New York: The Crossroad, 2001), 40
[92] Bénézet Bujo, *Foundations of An African Ethic*, 85.
[93] Dominique Nothomb, *"Signification Religieuse des Récits,"* 112.

strictly from the ritual celebration, from the consecration to Lyangombe through initiation that leads to the happy life. It is a gift as Nothomb adds,

> There is a radical humility to receive happiness that has not been deserved, that one can receive only from another who has been consecrated and who is trusted in total fact. Such an attitude does not lack religious promotion. Salvation exceeds possibilities of man, even those of his virtue and merits.[94]

But why did belief in Lyangombe become so viral among Banyarwanda? The environment in which Lyangombe arose corresponds to the African area that historians call "the domain of *Bami*" (kingdoms). The Bami (kings) were pastoralists, living in an area comprising about fifteen kingdoms where inequality, domination and submission were based on a hierarchy of three castes, the Lords (pastors), the servants (farmers), and untouchable hunters.[95] They were constituted of most of the population affected by misery and were even considered poor-minded.[96] Lyangombe abolished castes and kingdoms. His followers recognized him as the only king because he advocated the equality of all. For him there was neither rich, nor poor, nor castes, nor sexes. The heroes of Lyangombe accepted both male and female, regardless of one's social status, regional or ethnic origin. He fought for the suppression of an unequal society and against any injustice. [97] In addition, equality, and freedom (liberation) go together in the cult of Lyangombe. So, during the major or second-degree ordination, the main celebrant representative of Lyangombe shows the country to the initiate by saying: "Where you go, know that you are at home in this kingdom ... no one will therefore oppose your intention."[98]

The differences in the ritualized sex are also explained by imitation of Lyangombe hero, who seems to have systematically violated the taboos governing sexuality. In some stories, Lyangombe dies because he acts sexually as a free man. He was defeated because of his being seduced by a woman out of wedlock and met her in the forest.[99] It is also said that he begot Binego, his elder

---

[94] Ibid., 113.
[95] Melchior Mbonimpa, *Guérison et Religion* ..., 61.
[96] Gahigi Gérard "Ryangombe et la Société" *In Ryangombe, Mythe et Rites. Actes du Deuxième Colloque du Ceruki,* (Bukavu, Democratic Republic of Congo: Ceruki, 1976), 117.
[97] Ibid.
[98] Ibid.
[99] Ibid.

son, with a young girl who was still living with her family despite the opposition of the latter.

In contemporary sexual ethics, such a chauvinist decadence should not be adopted. To maintain positive aspects in Lyangombe cults does not suggest canonizing him as paradigmatic model of healing in the current Great Lakes region of Africa. Lyangombe cults implied transgression of sexual prohibitions in both language and deeds. It is observed that Western researchers who have been interested in Kubandwa cults as an integral component of the ceremonies of consecration to Lyangombe noted its vile aspect such as sexual relation during festivals. Within this sect, sexual ethics was marked by indecency and inequity. The violation of moral taboos was punished by capital punishment especially for women. In the modern Sub-Saharan Africa, holding such violation of human rights, patriarchal domination and sexual indecency represent a source of many evils and diseases for individuals, families and for the society. This should not be accepted.

Nevertheless, the healing rituals in the cult of Lyangombe offered a political motivation. According to the writer Paul Del Perugia, the kings tolerated such an underground society without ever ceasing to pay attention on it: "The wisdom of the princes of Rwanda discerned this small center of mysterious men. Not being able to include them in a state organization because, by their nature, they were allowed to live in clandestine societies"[100] Del Perugia insists on the mistrust of the kings which incited them to maintain some control over the sect. The kings remained cautiously away from Lyangombe elect. They tolerated their existence among good citizens, they did not take their grand master to court for performing mystical rituals. Every morning the kings publicly made a tribute of fidelity. Difficult to grasp, the sect of Lyangombe become for the people's representatives better to hold than to reject.[101]

The cult of Lyangombe and *Kubandwa*[102] were also used by kings to disqualify the pretenders to the throne. "The mere fact of being initiated was a

---

[100] Paul Perugia Del, *Les Derniers Rois Mages*, 221.

[101] Perugia Del Paul, *Les Derniers Rois Mages*, 223.

[102] Eric Heusch understands *Ukubandwa* as cults of initiation to spirit possession. The cults seem to have been promoted by the so-called Hutu tribal group which was subjected to unbearable socio-economic situation. The Kubandwa was most common in the central and the Southern part of Rwanda. Hunted by Catholic missionaries, the cult started disappearing in 1949. It was from that time considered as paganism, a disorder to the public good, and banned by the government which was religiously Catholic-inclined. The *Imandwa*, the people who perform Ukubandwa were promised by Ryangombe a new eschaton, a life of happiness in the present world and in the after-life. See Luc de Heusch, "Mythe et Société Feodale. *Le Culte du Kubandwa dans le Rwanda Traditionnel. Archives de Sociologie des Religions*, no.18,1964,136.

departure from the royal power, to live as sovereign and give the initiation to young princes and keep them away from the succession."[103] At the same time the cult to Lyangombe is politically defiant because of its origins. Without going so far as to assume that the hero himself was a citizen, Paul Del Perugia argues that the sect "came out of from the deep *Bantu*," that it regrouped a minority of mystical laborers and that it existed independently of the kings."[104] This is why this sect was able to propose to the various groups of the society to get out of their historical conflicts.

The Lyangombism elect were a little group and people adhered to it for some major reasons: hope in attainment to happiness, hope in reaching to a good health, redemption from trials that endanger all life, but also the search of honor and recognition. All initiated people to Lyangombism are promised a happy after-life, and among them, the names of the kings, princes, great ministers, and his elect were encoded in the luxurious archives, in the annals, in the monuments of the stories.

Today Lyangombism is not common. It was hardly to survive the Catholic profound belief by which, *Extra Ecclesiam Nulla Salus:* "Out of the church, there is no salvation."[105] Lyangombe and its followers were tracked down and banned wherever the Church settled in the Great Lakes region of Africa. Yet, there are today some Lyangombe followers, living a double belief of Christianity and traditional religion, especially in northern Rwanda and in the neighboring countries, Uganda and Burundi.

While a Christian interpretation may still tend to consider "the earth as a valley of tears" (Ps 84: 6) where the days of human being are numbered (Ps 90: 10) and misfortune because of sin, and therefore as punishment, Lyangombe promises good health to his elect in earthily life in the life after-death, not as a reward for the virtue and merits, but as a free offer. Healing of Lyangombe is not reserved to only heroes, it is opened to the simple ones who receive initiation. The spiritual initiation attracts those which the society despises and

---

[103] Perugia Del Paul, *Les Derniers Rois Mages*, 223.

[104] Ibid.

[105] The statement "out of the Church there is no salvation is found in many Church Fathers, Popes statement and theologians' statement, especially before Vatican II. Thomas Aquinas in 12th century compared the Church as the Ark of Noah, and that there is no salvation out of the Church. In the Encyclical Letter, *Quanto Conficiamur Moerore*, August 10, 1868 (paragraph 7), Pope Pius IX said that it would "a grave error" to think that "men who are living in error" (…) "can attain eternal life." For sub-Saharan Africans who embraced Christianity from the beginning of 19 century, one of the errors the missionaries found was syncretism, mixing of traditional rituals and Christianity. *Lyangombism* and other local religion were thus contested.

disqualifies, the lower classes and women. Nevertheless, like any secret society, Lyangombe does not include of course everyone, which seems a contradiction in terms. There is a certain elitism, but its originality and success lied in welcoming the elect out of tribal and caste systems. The elect of Lyangombe came from any social layers of society, including the impoverished ones.

Lyangombism infiltrated the Great Lake region of Africa in fifteenth century and Christianity settled in twentieth century. Today Lyangombe's social influence has been conquered by Christianity and Islam. Lyangombe's spiritual healing monopoly has largely been taken by the established religions, especially Christianity which settled in Africa in the twentieth century. As a Rwandan proverb would say "a blessing which comes from above spreads everywhere."[106] Once Christianity in Africa was embraced by kings[107] their subjects followed. This includes the populace of all social strata, without distinction of ethnic groups, of social classes, of sexes, and it has the advantage of sending its message through a spectrum of many believers rather than to a few elects. This leads us to the fourth section, with a focus at Christianity and its spiritual healing message.

1.4. CHRISTIANITY AND SPIRITUAL HEALING POWERS

The search for healing and health we just came to explore among the followers of traditional religion in Rwanda is ever today seen in Rwanda and in Africa at large, sometimes by means of very aggressive pietism and intolerance against traditional religion. A Catholic bioethical perspective is required to help us discern healing powers of Jesus of Nazareth in sub-Saharan Africa.

A thousand years before the coming of Christianity in Africa, religious healing was trusted in addressing human ailments. Scholars refers to the *Ebers*

---

[106] Kinyarwanda transposition of the proverb *"Umwera uvuye ibukuru ukwira hose"*
[107] According to historians, by 1900 the 1st the White Fathers (The Missionaries of Africa) arrived in Rwanda, bringing Christianity to native Rwandans. The group included Monsignor Jean Joseph Hirth who visited king Yuhi Musinga in February 1900. These missionaries talk about religion inclusivity among other issues and were given a land to start the first mission at Save, South Rwanda. The following year, the same king who was then becoming hostile to Christianity was deposed by Belgian colonists. His son Rudahigwa was enthroned and was named Mutara III Rudahigwa. The later king welcomed Christianity and was baptized (Charles Léon Pierre) on October 1943 with his mother Nyiramavugo and his wife Gicanda by Mgr Leon Classe. The conversion of the king fueled among the rest of native citizens a sense of trust and conviction that Christianity becomes the religion of the kingdom to be followed. People massively abandoned Lyangombe and come to the baptismal font. See Lamarchand Rene, Ian Linden, "Church and Revolution in Rwanda" *The International Journal of African Historical Studies,* 1978, vol.11 (2), 368. See also https://www.newtimes.co.rw/section/read/111084 accessed on February 21, 2019.

Papyrus in ancient Egypt which existed around 1552 B.C.[108] The document mentions the laying on of hands to medical treatment:

> If you treat a man for a gaping wound in his head…you must probe his wound. Should you find there something uneven under your finger…if you treat a man for a fracture in his cheek, you must put your hand on his cheek in the fracture."[109] …While this practice of laying hands on the sick persons was used as a diagnostic of diseases, it refers to todays' religious laying on of hands for conferring blessings and healing.[110]

Out of Africa, the Greeks used healing touches in the Asklepian temples as a remedy to sickness. The philosopher Aristophanes talks of the use of hands in the Athenian city as a therapy for blindness.[111] In addition to people who performed healing by laying hands, there are sacred places in the early times of Christianity until today which have been considered as having healing powers. The pool of Bethesda referred to in the Gospel of John 5, where people used to plunge to be healed is one among many examples in the antique world.

Christianity in the West, in Europe, and in the Americas, has seen many places where people go as pilgrims with hope to be blessed and healed. The healing miracles which happen at the shrine of Our Lady of Lourdes in France and at Our Lady of Fatima in Portugal are widely documented. Medical and theological studies have so far confirmed 69 patients who have been healed among several thousand people who went to Lourdes in search for healing.[112]

The search for healing is found among both Catholic and Protestant Christians. Protestant healers are known John Alexander Dowie, Emmanuel Movement and Peculiar People a group founded in London in 1836 by John Banyard who refused medical treatment as an article of faith. In America, there are Christian groups such as the Seventh Day-Adventist, Christian Scientists,

---

[108] E. Gemi-Iordanou, et al, eds. *Medicine, Healing and Performances* (Oxford—Philadephia, Oxbow Books), 33.

[109] Ibid.

[110] Ibid.

[111] See Karellissa V. Hartigan, *Performances and Cure: Drama and Healing in Ancient Greece and Contemporary America* (London – Sidney: Bloomsbury, 1988), 13.

[112] See Bernard Francois et al, "The Lourdes Medical Cures Revisited": https://www.ncbi.nlm.nih.gov/pmc/articles/PMC3854941/pdf/jrs041.pdf, The Cure at Lourdes Which have been recognized as miraculous by the Church." http://www.miraclehunter.com/marian apparitions/approved_apparitions/lourdes/miracles1.html. Accessed on December 10, 2018; James Bishop' Theological Rationalism: https://jamesbishopblog.com/2016/11/02/medical-bureau-confirms-69-miracle-healings-at-lourdes/ accessed on December 02, 2018.

Mormons, Jehovah's Witness and Pentecostals.[113] Mary Baker Eddy (1821-1910) founded a group aiming at healing experiences. There are women healers such as Maria B. Woodworth Etter (1844-1924), Aimee Semple McPherson (1890-1944), and Kathryn Kuhlman (1907-1976).

Most Christians claim the possibility of miracles with reference to biblical texts. Yet the understanding of miracles should go beyond a literal reading of the scriptures. Scholars think that Jesus may have performed miracles of which faith healing represents a major dimension. Note that Jesus's healing miracles do not necessarily mean sickness or diseases he healed are impossible to address by natural or scientific medicine. In what follows we rely on Barry L. Blackburn and Daniel Harrington, John P. Meier, and Gary Ferngren, in discerning the meaning of healing according to Jesus and Christianity. We highlight that faith-healing cannot be conceived without compassion and reaching out to the impoverished ones.

Barry L. Blackburn in *Cambridge Campion to Miracles* recognizes several miracles: seven exorcisms, and thirteen healings in the Synoptic Gospels.[114] By writing the Gospels, "evangelists regarded Jesus's miracle working as a major aspect of his work"[115], as adds Bary L. Blackburn.

In Harrington Daniel's *Jesus A Historical Portrait,*[116] healing miracles and Jesus's compassion are related. Harrington asks: Do Jesus's miracles represent an historical reality? Did he really resuscitate Lazarus? What do miracles signify to Jesus and what did his miracles mean to the early Church? Thus, how could we understand them today? Harrington's questions help us to unpack the connection of Jesus's healing and compassion.

As Daniel Harrington suggests, Christ as a healer does not mean a medical practitioner but rather a miracle worker.[117] Harrington refers to the Gospels, on their reports of miraculous activities. Almost one third of Mark's Gospel is devoted to Jesus' miracles. The fourth Gospel contains also seven miracles known as "signs" including the wedding of Cana, the raising of

---

[113] Melchior Mbonimpa, *Guérison et Religion en Afrique* (Paris: Harmatan, 2012), 15.
[114] Barry L. Blackburn, "The Miracle of Jesus": *Cambridge Companion to Miracles*. Graham H. Twelftree, ed. (Cambridge: Cambridge University Press, 2011), 114.
[115] Ibid.
[116] Daniel J. Harrington, *Jesus: A Historical Portrait*. Cincinnati, OH: St. Anthony Messenger, 2007), 37.
[117] Ibid.

Lazarus from the dead. In the four Gospel, Harrington counts seventeen healings, six exorcisms and eight nature miracles.[118]

What does a miracle mean? In the Harrington's view, a miracle is "an event that is an exception to the laws of the nature."[119] The Bible describes miracles as "signs and wonders" acts of power that are attributed to God.[120] The Old Testament talks of miracles performed by Moses's leadership, when the people of Israel traversed the Jordan River in the book of Exodus. The Bible also refers the wondrous deeds performed by prophets Elijah and Elisha and other prophets.

John P. Meier, a New Testament scholar, suggests that a miracle has three aspects: "(1) It must be an unusual event that can be perceived by others. (2) It has no natural explanation. (3) It appears to be the result of an act of God."[121] The evangelists seem to have no doubt that Jesus performed miracles. Jesus himself, in the words of the evangelist Luke, attests to exorcise and heal as he says, "if it is by the finger of God that I cast out the demons, then the kingdom of God has come to you" (Luke 11:20). His own private and public life was marked by miraculous events, including his spiritual conception, his baptism, his transfiguration, and his death. These considered, how are we to interpret Jesus's miracles? Scholars suggests three aspects.

First, Jesus'miracles are signs of the kingdom of God. Barry L. Blackburn sees the significance of Jesus's exorcisms, healings, and revivifications as pointers of the coming of the Kingdom of God.[122] The kingdom of God suggests people to repent and believe, it gathers all religious and social strata at the table of fellowship, welcoming the poor and outcast, the oppressed, it heals the evil possessed ones and gives healing touches to the sick. Jesus operated miracles acknowledging that the Spirit of God is upon Him, he is the anointed one to preach the good news to the poor…to heal the broken hearted to preach deliverance to the captives and recovery of the sight to the blind, to set the oppressed free.[123]

---

[118] Daniel J. Harrington, *Jesus: A Historical Portrait*, 37.
[119] Ibid., 38.
[120] Ibid.
[121] John P. Meier as cited in Daniel Harrington, *Jesus: A Historical Portrait*, 38.
[122] Barry L. Blackburn, "The Miracles of Jesus" *Cambridge Companion to Miracles*. Graham H. Twelftree. Cambridge—New York: Cambridge University Press, 2011), 128.
[123] Luke 4:18

Jesus's mindfulness that he possessed a Spirit-given charism does not mean that he was spirit-possessed as claim African spiritual healers. Jesus's works goes far beyond what traditional healers perform. Some traditional healings are tainted by use of magic and obscurities. As Meier demonstrates, Jesus did not do magical or magnetic miracles as dubbed by some of the modern people.[124] E.P. Sanders suggests, Jesus's miracles were performed to "legitimize himself as a special figure in God's plan" who spoke for God. This was not a self-affirmation or vainglory. Occasionally, Jesus refused to show a sign from heaven, "Jesus declined to heal the curious or skeptical but was giving help to those who believe"[125]

Jesus likely believed himself not only to be one called by God to announce the coming of the kingdom of God, but also to be the agent through whom God would inaugurate his reign. When accused of exorcism via sorcery, Jesus is reported to have replied: 'But if it is the Spirit of God that I cast out demons, then the Kingdom of God has come to you' (Mt 12:28; Lk11: 20) This *logion* appears to mean that Jesus believed that through his exorcisms God was acting against the tyranny of Satan and his demons to inaugurate his eschatological reign.[126]

In the view of Barry L. Blackburn, by operating miracles, Jesus considered himself as Spirit-anointed as announced in book of Isaiah 61:1. As Isaiah prophesied, the job of Messiah was clear: To proclaim release to the captives and recovery of sight to the blind, to let the oppressed go free. As to why Jesus's healings are associated to exorcisms, on one hand, is because Jesus's exorcisms resulted in physical healing, on the other hand is that there was an expectation on the behalf of Jewish contemporaries that the coming of God's reign will conquer Satan and the demonic, as the Old and the New Testaments account (Dan 5:10-11; Mt 9.29).[127] The coming of the reign of God was seen as a time to bind Satan, to crush demons, to free human being imprisoned in its malice.[128]

What I have described above contends that Jesus exorcised, healed and resuscitated the dead for He believed that God called Him to proclaim and realize God's reign both in his words and in his deeds. The proclamation of the

---

[124] Meier refers to Gerd Theisen and Annette Merz who respectively dubbed Jesus' Miracles as magical miracles and charismatic miracles.
[125] Barry L. Blackburn, *The miracles of Jesus*, 121.
[126] Ibid.
[127] Ibid., 122.
[128] Ibid.

kingdom of God is all-encompassing. It includes calling sinners to conversion and forgiveness, it calls people to be reconciled with God, with themselves and with the creation as a whole; the kingdom of God heals the human race from its vice and actualizes the beatitudes which promise happiness to the poor. The kingdom of God is an invitation to come out from death to life and from captivity to freedom, it defies all personal and societal forms of oppression and violence against the marginalized and the poor; it resists all structures that rear greed, abuse, and enmity. In the language of Pope Francis, the kingdom of God goes against "the culture of death."[129]

As Barry L. Blackburn notes, Jesus firmly believed and ministered as one called to bring the good news of the kingdom of God to the poor, and to encourage generosity toward the destitute. His miracles of healing and deliverance should be interpreted as compassion toward the poor.

One can see a correlation between illness or disease and poverty. Drawing this connection from the Scriptures, especially Isaiah 61.1-2; Luke 4.18-19, Blackburn is right to say: "Illness interferes with income-producing work, and doctors' fees could spell ruin (Mk 5.26)." Jesus' healing miracles were motivated by His virtue of compassion and mercy toward the poor and the suffering people as the Scripture attests. The people of God had an expectation to be redeemed by the God of compassion and mercy. Jesus' active compassion was accounted by evangelists, by welcoming people and feeding with his Words and breads (Lk 9:11 ff), by exorcising evil spirits (Mk 5:1 ff), by healing the social-excluded lepers (Mk1:41 ff), by giving comfort to the mourning (Lk 7: 11 ff.). Not only was Jesus compassionate but he taught people to be and do likewise.

To the rich young man who asked Him what he could do to receive the kingdom of God, Jesus replied: "Go and sell your possessions and give them to the poor" (Lk 12:33). In his teaching on the good Samaritan, Jesus invites us to care for our neighbors (Jn 4:9). Perhaps the most poignant passage which shows God Father in his Son as a paradigm of compassion, with mercy that heals our spiritual and physical misery is the prodigal Son (Mt 18:27). The compassionate God who saw his repentant son from afar was seized by mercy. He ran toward him, embraced him, and covered him with his arms on his neck. Not only the son felt reintegrated in the family, but he recovered his vital forces. Compassion has healing effects, it can restore one from loneliness to family and social life, it

---

[129] See Pope Francis, *Letter of His Holiness Pope Francis to the People of God*. Vatican City: Libreria Editrice Vaticana, August 20, 2018. http://w2.vatican.va/content/francesco/en/letters/2018/documents/papa-francesco_20180820_lettera-popolo-didio.html. Accessed on February 19, 2019.

consoles and brings hope. Compassion binds us together with Christ who came to give us life at full (Jn 10:10).

In what follows, we need to examine exorcism and faith-healing as as a Christian dimension in search for healing, but which need to be coupled with realistic efforts of biomedicine in sub-Saharan Africa.

1.5. Looking for a Realistic Approach

A prosperity Gospel interpretation of the scriptures which has permeated Catholic renewal in Africa would easily see Jesus and his disciples as compassionate healers who invite us today to lay hands on the sick persons so that they may recover health. Catholic ethics calls for faith enlightened by reason, and prayer for healing does not replace medical cures. In what follows, we rely on Gary B. Ferngreen's book, *Medicine and Religion*,[130] underlining that Christianity considers prayer and medicine as ways to witness our compassion and care towards sick persons.

Although Jesus was considered as a miraculous healer, in the views of Ferngreen "the early Christians did not believe that miraculous healing was normative in the treatment of illness. This is suggested by the fact that outside the narrative of Jesus' healings one finds little reference to it in the New Testament.[131] Ferngreen adds that Acts narrates few healings and attributes them to Jesus' disciples (Acts 8:3-10).[132] Miraculous acts were in other terms called "signs and wonders," *semeion* in Greek, and understood as authentication of God's power which accompanied the disciples and apostles (Acts 4:3).

Unlike frequent mentions of Satan and demons in the Gospels, most diseases healed by disciples were attributed to natural causes rather than demonic.[133] There are numerous evils related to nature, including phenomena which affect human health, and which are not necessarily demonic. In the New Testament, the Epistles which predate the writing of the Gospels rarely mention miraculous healing or demonic possession. If one could see the Gospels as an evidence of the coming of the messianic era with miracles performed by Christ, the dearth of miraculous performances among early-Christians could be an indication that the early followers of Christ assumed a realistic approach of

---

[130] See Ferngreen Gary B. *Medicine & Religion: A Historical Introduction.* Baltimore, MD: Johns Hopkins University, 2014.
[131] Ibid. 77
[132] Ibid.
[133] Ibid., 82.

faith-healing.[134] One could find in the Epistle of James a call for religious healing, with the elders called to anoint the sick and intercede for one's recovery (James 5: 14-15). It is however not clear whether the recovery expected is spiritual or physical. While the physical healing is much more supported by many interpreters, James'earlier verse (5:11) alluding to the perseverance and patience of Job could suggest a spiritual healing rather than physical. Still, it is rare to find apostles or disciples who were drawn to be healed miraculously.

The beloved friends of Paul, Epaphroditus (Phil 2:25-27) and Trophimus (2 Tim 4:20) "were not healed at all."[135] Although one could give it a spiritual interpretation, the apostle Paul, a healer he was, remained awfully suffering from a thorn in the flesh (2 Cor. 12:7-10). As Ferngreen suggests, this "may have been a physical disability that was never healed."[136] The apostle Paul gives some advice to his child in faith, Timothy, to take a little wine for the good of his stomach (1Tim 1:23). These examples show that the ordinary means of healing such as conventional medicine, folk or traditional cures were favored and promoted in lieu of religious healing. [137]

Within Catholic tradition, the early Church fathers discerned healing with delicacy. While believing in miraculous healing, Athanasius, Ambrose, Jerome (c. 374-420), John Chrysostom and Augustine of Hippo (347-407) believed that sickness was merely one aspect of the material evil that had arisen from the Fall.[138] They looked on illnesses as the result of natural, if providential, causes that could be treated by physicians or other healers, of whom a broad spectrum existed in the medical marketplace of the classical world. The theologian Origen of Alexandria in Egypt (185-254) upheld medicine "as beneficial and essential to humankind."[139] Tertullian who used many medical analogies in his writings, recommended Christians to use conventional medicine. Jesus Christ was allegorically called the great physician (*Christus medicus*), meaning that Christ is the Savior of sin-sick souls, not merely of physical healing.[140]

As Imagogie suggests, Christ's powers to heal could reasonably help Africans to look for him in all times, including of course in times of crises and

---

[134] Ibid., 77.
[135] Ibid.
[136] Ibid.
[137] Ibid.
[138] Saint Augustine as cited by Gary B. Ferngren, *Medicine and Religion*, 78.
[139] Origen as cited in Gary B. Ferngren, *Medicine and Religion*, 78.
[140] Tertullian as cited by Gary B. Ferngren, *Medicine and Religion*, 78.

sickness.[141] As Robert. E. Moses suggests, devoting energy and spiritual warfare "is to fail to come to grips with the power of the resurrection, which is the assurance for Christians that evil powers will never have the last word against God's people."[142]

CONCLUSION

Six core aspects could be drawn from what I have developed in this first chapter.

First, the investigation of the African worldview has helped to grasp that the latter did not come in a void. As the Jesuit Eric de Rosny underlines, the efficacy of African healing could be seen in its approach to bring the patient in the web of spiritual and social relationships, in a healing liturgy; considering healing principles of the forests, of community and family, of fire, of herbs and barks, of taking the soul to "a mysterious relationship with God, with ancestors and spirits."[143] Addressing skepticism as regards to spiritual healing, Eric de Rosny adds

> No rational system can exhaust the mystery of life and death, or health and illness. You cannot deny the existence of sorcerers when experience clearly shows that certain persons have the power to make their neighbor fall and die.[144]

Second, I have demonstrated that African healing in the Great Lakes region of Africa came from social and personal dangers of diseases, of poverty and domination, of an unequal society governed by kings and colonialists who exploited and subjugated the poor and the outcasts. Such structural ills against the poor represent a culture of death which must be resisted and hopefully healed.

Third, I have mentioned Lyangombe as a traditional and spiritual healing hero, pointing out the roots of spiritual healing, the recourse to ancestors and beliefs in the divine healing powers as a social symptom of poverty, the need for

---

[141] Imagogie as cited by Robert Ewusie Moses. *Practices of Power*, Minneapolis, MN: Fortress Press, 2014), 223.
[142] Robert E. Moses, *Practices of Power*, 233.
[143] Eric de Rosny is a French Jesuit worked in Douala, Cameroun. His accounts of immersion in the world of African traditional healing is found in his book, *Healers in the Night*. Maryknoll, N.Y: Orbis, 1985. See Eric de Rosny, Healers in the Night (Maryknoll, N.Y: Orbis, 1985), 197.
[144] Eric de Rosny, *Healers in the Night*, 201.

compassion, inequality, a social and personal cry of sick-poor people and the outcasts. Within a population deprived from public health infrastructures, without quality medical personnel and essential medicines, it would not be surprising for people to look for divine powers and faith-healers.

Fourth, in keeping with Esther Acolatse, I have observed a persisting belief in the world spirit among Christian Africa, especially in Rwanda-Burundi. Without demeaning the possibility of evil spirits, I have opposed the attribution of evils and diseases to the spirit world which would run the risk of making Africans irresponsible agents. African Christianity today is called to deepen an understanding of spiritual powers, so that by the healing power of Christ they may resist and cast out malevolent spirits, and combat moral and social evils which eliminate, destroy African lives.

Fifth, I have underlined the efficacy of the healing power of Christ over evil spirits and demons. Christ's victory over evils spirits entails allowing the power of the Holy Spirit permeate within persons and structures. In keeping with saint Paul, Christian spiritual battle goes beyond one's flesh, one's blood, one's health. It is a fight against sin and death (Rom 7:14-25).

Sixth, I have stressed that Catholic ethics puts medicine at the center to treat diseases. While medicine strives to bring cure, many people stay uncured and in search for healing. Beyond African traditional healers, Catholic ethics confesses Christ as the Healer of the healers, not a medical doctor. Faith-healing in its various forms may support medical care, but it does not replace it. To take down sub-Saharan Africans from the cross of illnesses and diseases, both traditional-spiritual and scientific medical approach are doomed to failure without taking an integral and a holistic view of illness, biological, social, spiritual, historical, psychological. It is essential to emulate Christ who accompanies and heals the person with compassion, Christ who came to serve and not to be served, Christ who meet the poor and the outcasts in their most need.

CHAPTER II

FAITH-HEALING IN SUB-SAHARAN AFRICA

In this second chapter, I would like to explore the continuities of healing powers within African Catholic Christianity and their link with social, moral, medical, and political matters. The chapter illumines what we are ought to bring in as a Catholic bio-ethical and pastoral response to helping the sick and possessed (chapter III). We propose to achieve this by: 1) considering the importance of faith healing among African society; 2) sketching the development in healing and exorcism in Catholic teaching, a section in which I shall highlight an historical development in France and some other countries in the West considered to be at the forefront on Christianity in the Sub-Saharan Africa; 3) considering some cases of faith-healers in the Sub-Saharan Africa, persuaded that the charism of healing does not come in a void. The biographical data I present in the second section helps us realize the concrete reality lived by Catholic healers. Sickness and possession are not to be addressed by mere spiritual approaches, they call for multi-sectoral approaches: social, political, and medical approaches, and by accompanying and listening to each and all those affected personal and social evils. 4) I shall finally bring analysis of the cases as we highlight the views of the *magisterium* (Popes and local bishops) on Catholic exorcism and healing today.

2.1. WHY IS FAITH HEALING IMPORTANT IN AFRICAN SOCIETY?

Faith-healing as a theological issue within African Christianity amidst many other questions is in fact one of the themes that one could observe as both an ancient and a modern phenomenon, either openly or secretly. Neckebrouck Victor calls the problem "spontaneous inevitable, unconscious automatic inculturation."[145] One cannot always defend healing without seeing the healed or reduce healing claims to irrationality and enchantment. Faith-healing in Africa emerges from a context where life is extremely precarious, within a crushed and crucified people, craving for health and wholeness.

As Jean Marc Ela's *My Faith as an African* laments, the Sub-Saharan population faces death and threats from all corners: civil wars, HIV/AIDS, Ebola, terrorism, tribalism, sexual harassment, rape, hatred, and evils of all

---

[145] Victor Neckebrouck, *Paradoxes de l'Inculturation* (Leuven: Leuven University Press, 1994), 87.

sorts. The same author deplores: "We must question the demagogic use of slogans like "Health For All"! Within a society living on one cash crop, in poor housing, and with the dilemmas caused by development and globalization. Because of these factors, the society struggles to respond to problems of nutrition and health. Food shortages result not so much from natural calamities or disasters caused by climate as from policies of domination over the peasants.[146]

Within such tragic situations as psychosomatic trauma of the 1994 genocide in Rwanda, Christian liturgy within an ambiance of music, dramatic melodies, and dances creates a collective resistance, a haven for spiritual healing and possibly a physical one. The festive assembly works as a fence against the moral, mental, and perhaps even physical death. Singing, dancing, ornaments, participate in a kind of group therapy. Those who come to Church and healing rallies while broken-hearted come out hopeful for a better tomorrow, ready to strive for living.

Christian liturgy and sacramentals such as holy water and intercessory prayers thus present spiritual healing as a place for rescue from the snares of the evil one through celebration of life, in fostering hope and faith in God. As Gary R. Gunderson and James R. Cochrane's *Religion and the Health of the Public* argues, religion harbors tangible and intangible assets such as sacraments and rituals which can foster the health of individuals and communities through a mutual and communal accompaniment. Eucharistic and liturgical celebration become a conduit of vital forces, allowing expression, and sharing with others theirs joys and sufferings.[147] B. J. Turnock clarifies:

> People gather, they congregate. In the most basic sense, the gathered people accompany each other through their journey of life, even to its end. They show up in times of dependency, celebration, lament, learning, and loss. The acts of accompaniment are part of membership....one experiences accompaniment as the fruit of human association, as an affirmation of commonality, not dependency; one of the companies, one is accompanied. The faith forming entity has the peculiar strength of generating such associations across bounds of race, blood, class, party, and even distance that are crucial to the health of the community.[148]

---

[146] Jean Marc Ela, *My Faith as an African* (Maryknoll, NY: Orbis, 1989), 70.

[147] See Gary R. Gunderson and James R. Cochrane, *Religion and the Health of the Public: Shifting the Paradigm* (New York: Palgrave McMillan, 2012), 49.

[148] B. J. Turnock as cited by Gary R. Gunderson and James R. Cochrane, *Religion and the Health of the Public*, 104.

Faith and its manifestation through prayer and celebration may be an adjacent place for spiritual healing, and in some cases, for physical healing. In the African context, this requires a return to the source of Christianity, to contemplate Christ as the Supreme-Healer, not the ancestors; to search and find God who can provide health and wholeness in temporal life, who can use both natural and spiritual means to provide health to his creation, God who, above all, gives salvation.

African Catholic faithful and particularly ministers acknowledge the Christ of Nazareth, who lived in a context quite like that of present-day sub-Saharan Africa, amidst imperial domination and exploitation, at a time of great troubles and paradoxes, belief in occult forces, and antique healing remedies. Eventually He came to be recognized as a wounded-healer because he both healed those who suffered and suffered himself on their behalf.

A significant number of Catholic scholars have addressed the issue of healing and called for an ethical, pastoral, and theological answers. The theological solution invites us to give meaning to healing prayers so common in Africa among the charismatic or evangelical groups. These include the practices of laying on of hands which are performed in various Christian denominations. Among committed Catholic Christians, it involves also the use of the holy water, crucifixes, rosaries, official and unofficial novenas addressed to saints, the claim of miraculous prayers communicated through social media, great numbers of pilgrims who attend national Catholic shrines such as the Martyrs'shrine of Namugongo in Uganda, the Sanctuary of the apparition in Kibeho in Rwanda, the chapels of Merciful-Jesus in Ruhango and in Kabuga in Rwanda, the Saint Vincent Healing Retreat Center at Thika in Kenya, the Healing Waters in Nigeria and many other places in Sub-Saharan Africa.

2.2. CATHOLIC FAITH-HEALING: MAJOR DEVELOPMENTS

Healing by exorcism, as *The Catechism of the Catholic Church* describes, is performed "when the Church asks publicly and authoritatively in the name of Jesus Christ, that a person or an object be protected against the power of the Evil One and withdrawn from his dominion."[149] The same *Catechism* agrees that the charism of healing is bestowed by the Holy-Spirit to some people, yet even intense prayers do not heal all the sick. It states:

> The Holy Spirit gives to some a special charism of healing to make manifest the grace of the risen Lord. But even the most intense prayers do

---

[149] The *Catechism of The Catholic Church,* paragraph, 1673.

not always obtain healing all illnesses. Thus St. Paul must learn from the Lord that "my grace is sufficient for you, for my power is made perfect in weakness," and that the sufferings to be endured can mean that "in my flesh I complete what is lacking in Christ's afflictions for the sake of his Body, that is, the Church.[150]

More examples about the charism of healing by exorcism which needs a deeper interpretation, are found in the Old Testament and in the New Testament, especially in the books of Acts and, in the Gospels.[151] This has inspired the Catholic tradition from the early centuries.

Indeed, the warfare against the devil and evil is as old as humanity. Christians believe in God, and they want his creation to be exempt from the devil. It is from this perspective that early in the second century, exorcism was introduced in the rite of baptism, and Pope Hippolytus (170-225) imposed it on catechumens to keep them away from the influence of the devil. Exorcism was associated with the original sin, and it was binding on all baptized Christians. In 416 when Pope Innocent reserved the power of exorcism to priests and deacons by using holy water, oil, salt, and accompanied by the very Latin formula: *Vade retro Satana!* "Go back, Satan"[152]

The influence of Satan and the fallen angels (demons), as the Catechism of the Catholic Church recounts, were linked to heresies and Catholic Inquisition. The practice of exorcism spread between the twelfth and the eighteenth century.[153]

Laurent Amiotte-Suchet's article entitled: "A Ministry of Ritual Bricolage: A Case of A Diocesan Exorcist"[154] mentions the notorious demonic outbreaks which happened in the monastery of Loudun in France in 1634.[155] Some years earlier in 1614, Pope Paul V declared the *Exorcism Ritual*, and a *Manual of Exorcism of the Catholic Church* was published in 1626. The Manual

---

[150] The *Catechism of the Catholic Church*, paragraph, 1508.

[151] See 1 Sam 16-10; Mk 1:2-34; 3:20-30; 5:1-20; 9:14-29; Lk 11: 24-26; 13:32); Matthew 12: 24-28; Acts 2:1-13; 8:26-40; 10:44-48; 13:1-12; 19:11-20.

[152] In reference to the Gospel of Mark and Matthew (Mk 8:33; Mt 4:9)

[153] The notorious example is the episode of Loudun (Poitiers, France) in 1632. The Ursulines nuns were said to be possessed by demons and this became a popular story in Europe. The Church replied to the issue by sending a cohort of exorcists who performed theatrical rituals without casting the devil.

[154] Laurent Amiotte-Suchet, "Un Ministere de Bricolage Rituel: Le Cas d'un Exorciste Diocesain," *Ethnologie Française,* 2016/1, No.161, 117.

[155] Michel de Certeau, *The Possession at Loudun* (Paris: Gallimard, 1990), 11.

provided criteria[156] to identify possession as it calls priests to discern possession of mental illness from other diseases.

The 1900's came with conflicts of reason and faith. This was a time of the emancipation of reason. Everything must be examined by the court of reason: What is the devil? What is the meaning of evil? This was an era of advance in medical sciences, in psychiatry and psychology. Science got more light on the causes of dementia and epilepsy. Religious phenomena such as apparitions, and miraculous healing became doubted and even denied. The medical point of view was partially authorized by Church officials, who, as Bryan Wilson notes, are involved in secularization.[157] The practice of exorcism within the Church became problematical.

The middle-twentieth century brought new reforms related to the second Vatican Council (1962-1965): reform toward Protestantism, openness to liberal theologies, liturgical reforms, authority of the priests, the place of the laity, and other changes. The Council revised many ritual instructions including the ministry of healing through exorcism, which was then being ignored, and many other ritual practices such as pilgrimages to Marian shrines, healing prayers and exorcism among Catholic practices which were highly considered among the modern Catholic faithful.

Laurent Amiotte-Suchet observes that it would be unlikely on behalf of Catholic officials to question practices claimed by the faithful and supported by biblical and apostolic traditions. Yet in the aftermath of Vatican II, many bishops were reluctant to mission new priests to the exorcism ministry, leaving exorcists to steadily disappear.[158]

François-André Isambert's work shows the relation to the Vatican II reforms, of the ritual of the sacrament of the sick in 1972, which clearly takes on a more symbolic dimension.[159] We entered the era of spiritualizing the devil, what Danièle Hervieu-Léger calls "metaphorization of evil,"[160] where the devil becomes a symbol but not a reality.

---

[156] One could be recognized as possessed when speaking a language, he/she did not learn, he/she shows an extraordinary force, shows knowledge of things she is supposed not to know, or when vomiting strange things, such as blades, stones, living snakes, etc.

[157] Bryan Wilson as cited by Laurent Amiotte-Suchet, "Un Ministère de Bricolage Rituel: Le Cas d'Un Exorciste Diocésain. *Ethnologie Française*, 2016/1/ No.161 (124)

[158] Laurent Amiotte-Suchet, "Un Ministère de Bricolage Rituel..." 118.

[159] François André Isambert as cited by Amiotte-Suchet, "Un Ministere de Bricolage Rituel," 118.

[160] Danièle Hervieu-Léger, as cited by Amiotte-Suchet, "Un ministère de Bricolage Rituel" 118.

In line with Isidore Froc's *Exorcists,* Amiotte-Suchet argues that the trends of secularization in the 1970's, Christianity in the West and in the South has stayed to some extent affluent and prayerful. The persistence of the search for healing and exorcism are attested by incessant pilgrimages and gigantic Catholic prayers for healing, a phenomenon contrary to the so called "end of religion" or "death of God" assumed by some philosophers. The end of the 1970's showed the opposite of the latter assumption. The priests officially mandated in the ministry of exorcism were most of the time overwhelmed by the number of people in search of healing, and as a response, the Church did not hesitate to appoint new priests as exorcist ministers without counting charismatic lay people and priest-exorcists found in different dioceses in the South and in the West. Isidor Froc and Nicolas Leneuf assert that since the mid-1990's in French-speaking Switzerland and in neighboring France, almost all dioceses have had their official exorcists.[161] In keeping with this assertion, Monseigneur Berchier[162] declared in 2002: These exorcist-priests were named "so that there is no dispersion and because every priest cannot be an improvised exorcist."[163]

In 1999, the Congregation of the Sacraments and Divine Worship[164] responded to the issue by reviewing the official text of the Church concerning the authority of exorcism and adapted the *Manual* which had been used since 1626. The 1614's criteria earlier set by Paul V was reconsidered, inviting us not to confuse possession and mental illnesses. This new ritual in Latin, while restating evil as a personal being, furthered the risk of interpreting suffering within the lens of evil possession.

The Catholic Church has made new reforms in healing and exorcism. The Catholic bishops of France met in Lourdes in 2003 and committed to appoint an exorcist in each of their respective dioceses. For the bishops, exorcism includes accompaniment and spiritual support. Moreover, the modern exorcists brought a more nuanced perspective. Their academic formation is open to medical doctors, to psychotherapists, to theologians, to social workers, and to specialized educators and other specialties. Yet, as scholars observe, many young priests are reluctant to take on exorcism like the famous Roman Curia exorcist, Dom

---

[161] Isidor-Froc and Nicolas Leneuf as cited by Laurent Amiotte-Suchet, "Un Ministère de Bricolage Rituel," 118.

[162] Monseigneur Remy Berchier was the vicar general of the bishopric of Fribourg.

[163] Monseigneur Remy Berchier as cited by Laurent Amiotte-Suchet, "Un Ministère de Bricolage Rituel." 118.

[164] In Latin: *Congregation de Cultu Divino et Disciplina Sacramentorum,* is the Congregation of the Roman Curia that treats affairs pertaining to liturgical practices of the Western (Latin Church) as distinct from the Eastern Catholic Churches.

Gabriele Amorth (1925- 2016).[165] The latter published numerous books on exorcism and created an International Association of Catholic Exorcists,[166] which started in 1990.

Within the modern exorcism ministry, there is a growing interest of exorcists toward experts such as psychiatrists as collaborators in a holistic healing ministry and much more of an integration of spiritual accompaniment, psychological counseling, biosocial approaches, addressing inequities, compassion, and the preferential option for the poor as integral components for an authentic healing ministry.

As Isidore Froc states, exorcism is "not a magical power entrusted... by bishops." It is a service to welcome, to help, to give comfort, on behalf of the Church, to those who have been deprived of their independence to trust in themselves and in the God of love.[167]

Prayer may support healing but it is not enough. Jeanne Favret-Saada's study of the practices of witchcraft in Normandy in France discovered among the 1970's priests-exorcists that when a possessed person is sent to the exorcist, the priest refuses to interpret it as a possession, but assures the person that she or he will be kept in the priests' prayers, straying from the request brought to him, guiding the unfortunate to consult a psychiatrist for recovery.[168] The same claim is upheld by Danièle Hervieu-Léger, twenty years later, as he writes:

> To give those who claim to be possessed the signs of compassion and prayer, if necessary, the practical advice that will enable them to find a required therapeutic assistance with a doctor or a psychologist, remains the main objective most of the time. But it is rarely what the patient expects: they are addressed to the exorcist as to someone who is invested with a power, inseparable from a professional competence allowing him to control the supernatural forces.[169]

---

[165] See Laurent Amiotte-Suchet, "*Un Ministère de Bricolage Rituel,*" 118.

[166] See International Catholic Association of Exorcists, http://icaoe.weebly.com/membership.html

[167] Fr. Isidor Froc has been missioned for the ministry of Exorcism in 1982. He worked for twenty years in the psychiatry chaplaincy. He is the first French priest exorcist to refer to psychiatry in the ministry of healing. See Isidore Froc, *Exorcistes: Repères dans un Nouvel Age* (Paris: Plon/Mame, 1996), 1.

[168] Jeanne Favret-Saada, *Les mots, La mort, Les Sorts* (Paris: Gallimard, 1977), 17.

[169] Hervieu-Leger Danièle, *Le Pèlerin et Le Converti, La Religion en Mouvement* (Paris: Flammarion, 1999), 50-51.

Many scholars argue that the new movement of priest-exorcists is not a regression. It responds to the pervasive phenomenon of secularization. The modern exorcist-healers would encounter patients in Sub-Saharan Africa and in the West for whom psychosomatic diagnosis may not make sense, patients who believe in the real existence of the devil. This critical point brings into play the search for the meaning of the origin of evil and the ways to effectively address it. The works written by the exorcists themselves already allude to the challenge of this perspective. On the one hand, there is the trend to look at evil-possession as a mental problem or to give the devil a mere spiritual sense in the light of Fr. Isidore Froc. On the other hand, as Dom Gabriele Amorth[170] observes, there is a tendency to demonize priest-exorcists for their approach by bringing back belief in evil in reference to the hostility against the devil in early Christianity, in medieval times, and in the late twentieth century.[171]

Yet, are these approaches adequate? Would just seeing evil possession as psychosis or misery solve it? What does the life of the claimed exorcists and their ministry inform us about in today's Africa? What do the medical and social-political problems tell us? Would it not be irrational to simply "demonize" or "psychologize" exorcist-healers when they strive to help the sick and possessed persons? Still, although faith-healing is widely followed, the latter trends are not uncommon among Catholic believers, both in the West and in modern Sub-Saharan Africa. Such a perverse reality on the ground should not be ignored. Admittedly, there have been many and there are still many Catholic exorcists and healers in Africa. We can consider their life to discern the core motivations which led them into a healing ministry, retain the good things they are doing, and propose how their ministry should be improved to render it more effective.

2.3. HEALING IN AFRICAN CATHOLIC CHRISTIANITY

Unlike spiritual healing in the pre-Christian Africa which we discussed in the first chapter, faith-healing in the modern-evangelized Africa no longer seems to be a secret phenomenon. It engages different areas of society especially charismatic-lay persons, and clerics as well as their prelates. In this section, we

---

[170] Fr. Dom Gabriele Amorth, born in 1925, is a Catholic priest, exorcist at Vatican, doctor of Human Rights and Journalism. In his book, Amorth has witnessed more than 70,000 exorcisms from the time he was named as an exorcist at Vatican, Rome in 1986. See Dom Amorth, *Exorcisme et Psychiatrie* (Paris: Editions du Rocher, 2002), 1.

[171] Dom Gabriele Amorth, *Exorcisme et Psychiatrie* (Paris, Edition du Rocher, 2002), 5.

describe four cases of African Catholic pastors, drawing from their biographies as reflections of the personal, social-medical, and political reality lived by their own flocks. Our cases are arranged according to a chronological pattern, from the eldest to the youngest. They reflect a significant area of Sub-Saharan Africa, namely Cameroon in the West Africa, Rwanda-Burundi in the Great Lakes region, the Democratic Republic of Congo in Central Africa and Zambia in Southern Africa.

We do not pretend to obliterate the possibility of demoniac-possession or put away belief in healing powers which are well known in the Judeo-Christian faith and in the African religions. Again, we do not pretend to say that psychotherapy and bio-medical technologies are enough to address the complex issues which today are claimed by Africans, Americans, and Europeans, especially the poor and underprivileged, and with which the Church is concerned. The risk is to embrace scientism or naturalism, and even worse, spiritualism. We would like to be enlightened by Catholic teaching and suggest an effective way to healing. An empathetic consideration of healers as well as their patients is needed, including their personal development and their social and medical concerns which motivated them to serve the sick and the possessed.

2.3.1. MEINRAD PIERRE HEBGA IN CAMEROON (1923-2008)[172]

Meinrad Hebga was born on March 31, 1923 in Edéa, Cameroon. By 1940, his course of studies led him to the major seminary, studying philosophy and theology (1947-1948). He then went to Rome where he obtained a master's degree with a thesis on *Serapion of Thebes* (1948-1952). A member of the Society of Jesus (Jesuits), Hebga was ordained priest on December 22, 1951 in Rome. He studied the history and philosophy of the physical and mathematical sciences at the Paris Institute of Science. He also studied social sciences at *Institut Catholique de Paris* (1960-1961) and obtained a double degree. He studied psychopathology at the University of Sorbonne where he obtained his master's degree in 1965. His scholarship culminated in a doctorate in philosophy at the University of Rennes in 1968. He also studied Bantu Linguistics at Duquesne University of Pittsburgh, Pennsylvania, U.S.A.

Ethnologist, philosopher, and theologian by formation, Hebga served as a professor, a theologian and a healer (exorcist). In 1964, he taught Latin, Greek,

---

[172] See Meinrad Pierre Hebga' biography by Paulin Poucouta, *African Theology in the 21st Century: The Contribution of Pionneers*, ed. Benezet Bujo (Nairobi, Kenya: Pauline Africa, 2003), 70-74.

and Philosophy at Collège Libermann in Douala, Cameroon. From 1971-1984, he was a professor of anthropology at the Abidjan Catholic Institute, and was a visiting professor of theology at Loyola University of Chicago (1975-1976) and at the Weston Jesuit School of Theology (1977-1978). He taught anthropology at the Gregorian University, Rome. He also taught philosophy courses at John Carrol University in Cleveland, Ohio (1985). He returned to Cameroon and became a professor at the University of Yaoundé and at Institut Catholique of Douala, Cameroon.

Fr. Hebga was known in Cameroon and worldwide, particularly for his healing and deliverance ministry. This goes back to his encounter with the charismatic renewal he discovered in the United States of America in 1970, a Catholic prayer movement which he introduced to Cameroon and of which he became a leader. On September 30, 1976 Hebga started a charismatic group called *Ephphata* (Be opened) in reference to Jesus' healing miracle in Mark 7:34. The group was established in the village of Manguen, not far away from Yaoundé in Cameroon. *Ephphata* has today spread worldwide.

While a professor at John Carroll University, the charismatic renewal kindled in him an intense and fruitful pastoral activity. He received the sacramental of the effusion of Holy Spirit as a mark of integration into the Charismatic Renewal in 1976. This marked a decisive stage in Hebga's spiritual and pastoral life. Hebga went around the world giving conferences, lectures, and deliverance prayers. He breathed his last at the hospital in Château-Thierry on March 3, 2008.

African Catholic theology inherited from Hebga substantial publications to be considered in matters of healing and deliverance ministry. Among dozens of books he published, it is important to highlight:

(1) *Emancipation d'Eglises sous-Tutelle, Essaie sur l'Ere Post-Missionaire,*[173] an outstanding book which initiated reflections on African theology. Hebga calls for an African theology to carefully look into the diaconate of the ministry of the sick. For him, this has to be a multi-disciplinary task. The ministry of the sick has to rely above all on the Word of God and on the teaching of the Church. It needs to be enlightened by various sciences including medicine, psychopathology, psychotronics and physics. The author sees sorcery as a complex and challenging issue to discern, both on the level of reason and faith. For Hebga, denial should not be the solution.

---

[173] M. P. Hebga, *Emancipation d'Eglises sous-Tutelle, Essaie sur l'Ere Post-Missionaire.* Paris: Presence Africaine, 1976.

(2) Hebga's thesis on parapsychology entitled *"The Concept of Metamorphosis of Humans into Animals among Basaa People, South Cameroon,*[174] talks of the paranormal phenomena which seems like irrational, such as levitation, yet holds some reality of what people are living. He calls for a heuristic and pluri-disciplinary approach that deeply reflects on the issue. Hebga attempts to bring a rational answer in view of these paranormal phenomena prevalent in Sub-Saharan Africa. The African paranormal phenomena include apparitions, prophecies, visions, and witchcraft. For Hebga, we cannot discard such experiences prevalent in Africa and which are claimed by seeming reasonable people. It is not enough to concede that these phenomena are just beliefs and practices for certain tribes and cultures. This would be running the danger of relativism and even a cover-up. Africans need to know their own identity and so recover the religious and metaphysical beliefs which have been overpowered and barred by the encounter with Western philosophies and theologies. Beyond a denial of the paranormal phenomena, Hebga calls for Africans to face the paranormal phenomena and learn from them and so present a rational discourse which gives right to African reality.

(3) Hebga clarified his position by issuing *The Rationality of an African Account Paranormal Phenomena.*[175] Hebga maintains that it is not enough to pay attention exclusively to the external causes of diseases. It is essential, from an African viewpoint, to see how to fight against them, to consider sorcery as real. Hebga gives testimony of his own experience in the ministry of deliverance and healing with the Charismatic Renewal movement in Cameroun.[176] and answers the questions posed by this ministry.

In his other book, *Sorcery, Prayer of Deliverance,*[177] Hebga proposes an outline of prayers for exorcism and healing. He calls for prudence and delicacy, discretion without exhibitionism, but yet with a discerning spirit and conviction. For Hebga, priests and pastors ought to put again into practice this ministry of faith, of love and power willed by the Lord. God heals whenever he is prayed to. God may heal either physically or spiritually or both. God heals the person prayed for, according to the ministry of compassion and love.[178]

---

[174] See M. P. Hebga, *Le Concept de Métamorphoses d'Hommes en Animaux chez les Basa, Douala, Ewondo Bantu, Sud Cameroon.* Rennes, France: University de Rennes, 1968.

[175] M. P. Hebga, *La Rationalité d'Un Discours Africain sur Les Phenomènes Paranormaux.* Paris: L'Harmattan, 1998.

[176] M. P. Hebga, "Le Mouvement Charismatique en Afrique," *Etudes*, No.1-2 (1995), 67.

[177] See M. P. Hebga, *Sorcellerie et Prière de Délivrance. Refléxion sur Une Expérience.* Paris: Présence Africaine, 1968.

[178] Ibid.

2.3.2. EMMANUEL MILINGO IN ZAMBIA (1930-)

Among the widely known prelate healers in the African Catholic Church is bishop Emmanuel Milingo who became a renowned exorcist of the Catholic Church of Lusaka, Zambia (1970-1983).[179] He spent most of his time imposing hands on the called demon-possessed and on other sick persons. His ministry has however been opposed by the Holy See, he was criticized for neglecting the administration of his diocese, and he was ousted from its jurisdiction.[180] Milingo would be compared to the German Johann Joseph Gassner of the mid-eighteenth century[181] a priest who was believed to cast out demons in a poor area of south Germany.[182] Milingo was followed by thousands of Christians in Sub-Saharan Africa, in the USA,[183] and Italy.[184] His removal however was not the end of Catholic healers in Africa. Female and male lay persons as well as priest-figures continued to emerge; some claiming to have received the power to exorcise the possessed and others, combining spiritual, medical, and traditional healing powers.

2.3.3. FR. LÉOPOLD MVUKIYE (B.1954- IN BURUNDI)[185]

What is interesting in Fr. Leopold Mvukiye's healing ministry is a unique alliance of two religious' traditions, faith-healing and traditional medicine.[186] Fr. Léopold Mvukiye is a Catholic priest and a traditional-medical-healer. He is also a teacher at Buta minor seminary located in the province of Bururi, southern Burundi. He was born in 1954 in Vugizo, a town in the south of the country. After attending primary school in his native parish, he went to high school in Buta. Just before the end of high school in 1972, he suffered serious mental-related troubles caused by massacres in which he lost his father and

---

[179] Emmanuel Milingo, *The World in Between* (New York: Maryknoll, 1984), 2.

[180] See Adrian Hastings, *African Catholicism: Essays in Discovery* (London: SCM Press, 1989), 138.

[181] J. J. Gassner is a famous Catholic exorcist who was believed to cast out demons, especially in a poverty-stricken South German in the mid-1770. See Eric Midelfort, *Exorcism and Enlightenment: Johann Joseph Gassner and the Demons of Eighteenth-Century Germany* (New Haven: Yale University Press, 2005), 11.

[182] Ibid.

[183] Emmanuel Milingo, *The World in Between*, 10.

[184] Ibid, 11.

[185] The biography of Fr. Leopold Mvukiye is described by Melchior Mbonimpa, *Guérison et Religion en Afrique* (Paris: Harmattan, 2012), 81.

[186] Ibid, 81.

many members of his family. He accounts that he tried for more than three years with modern medicine without being healed. Later, his family took him to the house of a traditional healer who unknowingly contributed to his future ministry by orientating him to become a traditional healer.[187]

Recovered, he entered in 1975 at the Ecole Normale Supérieure in Bujumbura (E.N.S) and focused on Agriculture-Biology-Chemistry. The young man pursued his studies and graduated in 1980 with a thesis (mémoire) entitled An Inventory of Phytochemical Medicinal Plants of Burundi. He pursued studies of theology, first at the major seminary of Bujumbura, then at the Catholic University of Louvain-La-Neuve, Belgium. He was ordained a priest in 1989.[188] As a priest, he asked his bishop to practice the ministry of healing to reach out to his parishioners not only with the healing effects of the Word of God, but also with curative effects of medicinal plants. Mvukiye started practicing traditional medicine and healing gifts from 1990.[189]

Mvukiye's healing ministry combines teaching and caring for the sick. He obtained a house near the seminary that is used as a consultation room and a plot of land of two hectares for growing medicinal herbs. He became a committed priest who teaches during the days and does consults with the patients during the nights. The patients came to him from all corners of the country.

Since 2001, Mvukiye has presided over the Association of Traditional-Practioners in Burundi (ATRAPRABU) and has been as an influential personality who attends national and international talks on traditional medicine. In 2000, he represented Burundi at the Hanover International Fair, with a theme "Man, Nature and Technology."[190] In 2001 he participated in the Harare-Zimbabwe Symposium on the Integration of Traditional Medicine in African Health Systems.[191] In 2002 and again in 2003, he was invited by the Ethics Project of the University of Sudbury, Canada, as a specialist in Traditional Medicine.[192] The priest is known as a holistic healer. He has assimilated methods that have fallen into desuetude such as aromatherapy, which consists in treating diseases by plant scents or other scents such as burned skins.[193] In the

---

[187] Ibid, 81.
[188] Ibid, 82
[189] Ibid, 82.
[190] Ibid.
[191] Alain Cazanave Piarrot, "*Pratiques Sorcellaires et Crises Politiques au Burundi,*" http://geographica.danslamarge.com/Pratiques-sorcellaires-et-crises.html. Accessed on March 08, 2019.
[192] Ibid.
[193] Ibid.

post-civil war Burundi, Léopold fights against psychosis and traumatic problems.

What one would appreciate to Fr. Mvukiye is his study of diseases and the search for their cures through traditional-medical remedies. He acknowledges to have received the gift of healing through exorcism and the ability to identify those who engage in witchcraft. Mvukiye asserts that in the presence of witches, he could feel something like an aggression inflicted on his body, in his flesh, in his bones, in his bone marrow. From the beginning of what might be called his public healing ministry, Mvukiye claims to have the power of detecting the so-called witches, even those passing a mile away. It seems that on their side, witches also perceive the proximity of healers and must flee, sometimes screaming loudly to the great surprise of those who attend this uncommon show. After years in his ministry, Fr. Mvukiye notes a significant decrease of this witchcraft-sensing power. In his view, the activities of his center of traditional medicine has been taking all his time, and he has ended up lacking the freedom to pray as before.

As we consider Mvukiye's complex traditional-medicine and faith-healing approaches, it would be questionable to see him as a magician. The Southern-African Bishop's Conference which asks priest not to work as *Sangomas*[194] needs here our attention: "the belief that ancestors are bestowed with supernatural powers borders on idolatry, it is God and God alone who is all powerful while ancestors are created by him."[195] The American Catholic Bishops condemn the use of magical forces, sorcery, divination, Satan worship, and invoking the dead.[196] Mvukiye does not fall in these cases. Healing by divine grace and the healing by the powers of nature, including scientific medicine and the use of medicinal herbs are recognized by the Catholic Church. The Southern African Bishops stressed "the use of traditional herbal medicines and the eradication of diseases is not at issue. What is unacceptable is the use of magic, charms and recourse to ancestral spirits in rituals of healings."[197]

Nevertheless, the itinerary of Mvukiye has something in common with magicians. In his penetrating description of becoming an African shaman, Zahan Dominique affirms, "The African shaman is a character who joins to his remedies the gift of revealing witchdoctors and their actions. It is at the cost of a

---

[194] Sangoma are traditional healers in South Africa.

[195] See Southern African Catholic Bishop's Conference, *Ancestor Religion and the Christian Faith: Pastor Statement*, August 11, 2006.

[196] United States Conference of Catholic Bishops, *Guidelines of Evaluating Reiki as an Alternatives Therapy*. http://www.usccb.org/_cs_upload/8092_1.pdf.

[197] Ibid

long effort that shaman acquires the healing science. As a novice in the profession, he will practice day after day, he will start looking for a qualified teacher whose teaching he would follow for several years. Then he will undertake a true initiation at the end of which he will be admitted to heal."[198] Two elements can be mentioned:

First, *the initiation stage*. At the university and through learning from traditional healers of his own region, Mvukiye worked hard to master the science of herbs. With the traditional healer who cured his mental illness, Mvukiye had an experience of initiation. Additionally, in his life as a seminarian, Mvukiye lived a retreat-like, away from friends and relatives.

Second, he lived *solitude and withdrawal*. Zahan Dominique notes that witches disappear from the society by withdrawing into some remote and often dangerous places: seas, wildernesses, bushes, forests.[199] In the case of Catholic healers, withdrawal from society is equated to celibate life. While the magicians who disappear for years are considered as dead, in Africa where biological fertility is highly prized, celibacy is looked down on and is even seen as impossible. Those who make such a choice are on the one hand perceived as pretenders or socially dead, and on the other hand, they are seen as having healing powers. Antoine Rutayisire says: "I have well discerned not to become a priest who does not marry. Instead of becoming a Catholic priest who is unfaithful, running after women and committing adultery, I have gone where I'm allowed to marry."[200] Rutayisire's assertion is tainted by prejudice as it equates marriage with satisfaction of bodily desires and the search of earthly gains. He seems to reduce priesthood to moral decadence and deprivation. Some cases of priests who may have failed their call should not demean the essence of priesthood. While all the believers are priests by virtue of baptism, the Scripture acknowledges those "who made themselves so for the sake of the kingdom of God" (Mt 19:12). Priesthood finds its full meaning in Jesus Christ, our High-Priest (Hebrews 4:14), a compassionate Lord who heals the sick (Mt 14:14), who forgives all sins and heals all diseases (Ps 103: 2).

Coming back to Mvukiye as a priest-healer, his retreat created the demand and strengthened his fascination toward future clients. As a result, the poor, the afflicted, the sick, those starved for care, after many years waiting for one in

---

[198] Zahan Dominique, *Religion et Spiritualité et Pensée Africaine* (Paris: Payot, 1970), 159

[199] Ibid.

[200] Dr. Antoine Rutayisire is an outspoken Anglican pastor in Rwanda, known for biblical, cultural and political speeches in Rwanda. He is the head of African Evangelist Enterprise-Rwanda (A.E.E-Rwanda). His speech was translated from Kinyarwanda, available on https://mobile.igihe.com/abantu/interviews/article/. Accessed on February 11, 2019/

whom they believe to have an answer to their ailment, are glad and warmly accept his/her promising words, gestures and healing herbs. When medical remedies are lacking, the encounter with a priest-healer, a "eunuch for the kingdom of God." (Mt 19: 12) in Africa is highly trustworthy and valued.

The above description demonstrates that Mvukiye is a person who enjoys a rare experience of holistic healing. This does not imply that his healing is the model to follow. It could be appreciated for its combination of traditional-scientific and spiritual therapies. In a way, Mvukiye embraces an experience which does not entirely depend on natural powers and abilities. In his ministry, there is an integration of two religious traditions which are not necessarily incompatible, each of them allowing the expression of healing.

Yet Mvukiye's ministry has something to do with ancestral heritage while such a relation is questioned by the modern Christian population (non-Christians in Rwanda and Burundi are less than 10%).[201] Christian missions have condemned all that was related to African traditional religion. They even condemned valuable practices for healing. As Mvukiye notes, his patients were afraid of being lured against the Christian doctrine for which they would have to go to confession to other priests after receiving healing care from a traditional medical center. As mentioned above, it is during the nights that possession crises were diagnosed and treated. Amidst these dilemmas, Mvukiye seems persuaded of doing good yet without giving a rational explanation.

As a Rwandan proverb states, *Ijoro ribara uwariraye,* which translates "the night is accounted for by its guardian." The suffering is best explained by the sufferer. One would see the standing of Mvukiye as resulting from being a Catholic priest with a theological and scientific background. Additionally, his brokenness, sickness, and his scientific and theological training nurtured a sense of compassion and an active mind to reach out to those in need of better health. This follows what Henri J. M. Nouwen says: "We heal from our own wounds."[202] Our vocation to heal others is more often understood and performed by the broken-hearted than by the whole ones, and is, as Nouwen clarifies, rooted in Christ, the Wounded Healer who sends us to heal no other than the poor.

---

[201] http://www.pewforum.org/2017/04/05/the-changing-global-religious-landscape/ See also http://www.pewresearch.org/wp-content/uploads/sites/7/2010/04/sub-saharan-africa-appendix-b.pdf

[202] Henri J. M. Nouwen, *The Wounded Healers: Ministry in The Contemporary Society* (Garden City, NY: Doubleday, 1972), 5.

The Messiah, the story tells us, is sitting among the poor, binding his wounds one at a time, waiting for the moment when he will be needed. So, it is too with the minister. Since it is his task to make visible the first vestiges of liberation of others, he must bind his own wounds carefully in anticipation of the moment when he will be needed. He is called to be the wounded healer, the one who must look after his own wounds but at the same time be prepared to heal the wounds of others.[203]

As Nouwen also recalls, healing is more an invitation for one who has survived from mental, physical, and spiritual suffering, one who has gone through the shadow of the shadows, through a merciless fight against the forces of evil in the form of paralyzing terror, through the sadness that makes one mute, through all that blocks the human, what humiliates, crushes, kills.[204]

2.3.4. Fr. Ubald Rugirangoga (b.1956-d.2021 in Rwanda)

In 1961 Fr. Rugirangoga was five years old when he fled to the bush escaping from Hutu extremists who wanted to kill him. In 1963 at seven years old, his father was killed during murders against the Tutsi ethnic group in Rwanda. In 1973 Ubald, who was then at the minor seminary fled to Burundi in fear of extremist Hutu seminarians. He pursued his formation until 1978. He came back to Rwanda in the same year and joined the major seminary of Nyakibanda where he finished the first cycle of philosophy and theology. On July 4, 1984,[205] Ubald was ordained priest in the Cyangugu Diocese of Rwanda, where he ministered for ten years.[206] In his words "I felt in myself the desire to be a witness of Christ in the world."[207]

Rugirangoga survived the 1994's genocide of Hutu regime against Tutsi in Rwanda by fleeing to Democratic Republic of Congo. He says "I witnessed the genocide of Tutsi people all over in Rwanda, and by the grace of God, I miraculously escaped."[208] He fled to the Republic of Congo then to France until 1995, where he had intense moment of prayer, including pilgrimage to the Marian Shrine of Lourdes.

---

[203] Ibid. 82.
[204] Ibid
[205] Ubald Rugirangoga, *Forgiveness Makes You Free* (Notre-Dame, IN: Ave Maria Press, 2019), 51.
[206] Ibid., 52.
[207] Ubald Rugirangoga, *The Center of the Secret of Peace*, https://frubald.com. Accessed on 24 March 2019.
[208] Ibid.

Ubald went back to Rwanda in late 1995 and started a ministry of preaching forgiveness and reconciliation. In his words: "My bishop has been happy to consecrate me to serve God and his Church and to preach love and peace in a country that was so divided. My father has been killed simply because he was Tutsi; I was determined to preach and to live love in memory of my father and so many others who had died because of hate."[209] This was a time of the preparation for the jubilee of 2000 years of Christianity. It is within this perspective that the Church in Rwanda started a Synod of Reconciliation within Catholic faithful. Rugirangoga was appointed a permanent secretary of the Peace and Reconciliation Commission of the Cyangugu diocese.[210] Ubald recalls the letter issued by Archibishop Thaddée Ntihinyurwa in preparation for the feast of Jubilee,

> Rwanda: A dual Jubilee of Hope and Peace, ...we live today amid the turmoil of a cold war...where an atmosphere of permanent precariousness reigns. In this conflictual context, marked by the wounds of history, our path toward the Jubilee of the Year 2000 becomes hope and prayer. Hope for greater justice and peace, prayer for wounds to be healed and for reconciliation, accepting to forget the past to build a better future. [211]

The ministry of healing by Ubald is close to his profound suffering and compassion with people who were bewildered in the aftermath of genocide in search for inner peace, for a reconciled spirit, for hope to live. As in Jesus' time, Rwandans were like "sheep without a shepherd" (Mt 9:36) to whom a forgiving and compassionate heart can bring healing. Ubald states

> I came to see that it was precisely because I had endured these kinds of senseless loss myself that I was able to listen to the stories of so many others who died under these circumstances, simply because there was no compassion. This callousness reveals wounds that needed healing as well. And this is the work God is calling me to do.[212]

As Rugirangoga admits, people in Rwanda after genocide were living a cold war. There were "those who had lost their faith that no peace was possible until the full truth of what happened was out in the open, fully known and acknowledged among all people...Most of those who were closest to the events

---

[209] Ubald Rugirangoga. *Forgiveness Makes you Free,* 52.
[210] Ibid. 63.
[211] Ibid. 64.
[212] Ibid. 65.

were either dead or were determined to keep the truth quiet."[213] As a transitional justice, traditional Gacaca courts were opted for between 2002-2012,[214] and thousands of detainees suspected of perpetrating the genocide were released.[215] This has caused panic among genocide victims that those perpetrators then out of jails will come to kill them to eliminate the witnesses of their own crimes. People would go to Fr. Ubald with their anxieties and threats. Ubald, to respond to these crucial demands, started preaching retreats and recollections that brought hope to the anguished and wounded spirits.

Ubald accounts how he started healings prayers. He traces his charism of healing ten years before genocide when he started his priestly ministry in 1984.

> I was assigned in 1984 to be chaplain of the charismatic renewal movement in the Cyangugu diocese…God was already preparing me for the world of forgiveness and reconciliation I would be doing after genocide. He knew how many people would need these healing prayers, how many would need to be drawn back to Jesus after suffering so much pain, fear and sorrow. [216]

In 1987, amidst an outbreak of bacillary dysentery which conventional medicine was struggling to stop, Ubald would think: "If the doctors do not know how to stop this disease, we must ask God to stop this calamity!"[217] He invited parishioners to pray for the sick people at the end of every mass. While Ubald is uncertain whether this calamity was stopped by prayer, he confesses that "Jesus manifested his glory, power and mercy to his people…we prayed privately for people who we knew needed healing, without knowing whether or not the healing had taken place. But people returned from their doctors, claiming they had been healed; we praised God with them.[218]

In 1991, Ubald recalls having had a mystical experience of "a vision of a foot coming toward me, moving like a snake…then a voice told me that

---

[213] Ibid.

[214] According to Fr. Ubald Rugirangoga, Gacaca Courts were revived to give relief to the overburdened court system and restore a measure of peace to the community. Nearly two million cases were processed through this form of local mediation, in which community leaders listened to testimonies to determine the facts of each case. See Fr. Ubald Rugirangoga *Forgiveness Makes You Free*, 65.

[215] Ibid.
[216] Ibid. 93.
[217] Ibid, 94.
[218] Ibid. 94.

someone's left foot was suffering a wound that would not heal."[219] He heard also a voice telling him that someone was suffering from dizziness, another had an elbow pain, a pregnant woman needed assurance that she would carry her child to term. After the prayer, Ubald asked if there was anybody suffering from the sickness described in the vision. To his surprise, he would find them! "Together we gave thanks to God, and I urged them to confirm the healing with their doctors if they had not already done so." [220]

Ubald continued organizing charismatic retreats and healing prayers. Many people who attended would come back witnessing that they had met "Jesus who heals.[221] This was something new in the Catholic Church of Rwanda. The Catholic faithful started seeing in prayer, and especially in the most sacred sacrament of Eucharist, not only a place to refresh their spiritual life but also a divine milieu to get physical healing. The increasing number of Ubald's followers, both Catholics and non-Catholics was becoming an important issue that had to be handled by his superiors. Having in mind the experience of Bishop Milingo, Ubald could not perform this ministry without the permission of his bishop. As he met Mgr. Thaddée Ntihinyurwa in 1991, the then local bishop of Cyangugu diocese in Rwanda, the latter encouraged Ubald to go further in line with Acts 3:1-10 (the apostles healed the paralyzed man). However, the bishop advised him not to perform healing prayers in private chapels, but in the main sanctuaries of the Church.[222] As Ubald considers, there were many forms of suffering and sickness (psychological, spiritual, and physical) before the 1994 genocide against Tutsi.

> All these things took place in the years leading up to the genocide. For most of ten years I preached within my diocese and across my country about Jesus the healer. I saw many people receive physical healing and spiritual healing. I saw relationships healed and families reconciled, I saw many people open their hearts to Jesus and decide to reject evil and live only for him. Sadly, many of these people died in the genocide. While others gave in to the fear and hate that brought the genocide. Our Lady, while weeping many tears, warned us at Kibeho.[223],[224]

---

[219] Ibid.
[220] Ibid.
[221] Ibid.
[222] Ibid.
[223] See Fr. Ubald Rugirangoga, https://frubald.com. Accessed on 24 March, 2019.

What draws people to Fr. Ubald is at the same time his teaching on forgiveness and reconciliation, moral and social virtues which for him constitute the foundation of spiritual healing and possible physical healing. Marge Fenelon, a reporter for the *Catholic Herald* estimates the number who attend healing masses organized by Fr. Ubald in Rwanda. She says "it is not uncommon for 10,000-60,000 people to attend one of his healing masses organized in Rwanda."[225] Fr. Ubald thinks that healing starts from inside. It is a path which starts from one's spiritual life by forgiving and being reconciled. Ubald believes that Christ can heal those who adore him in faith: "if you are not healed spiritually, then the rest does not matter."[226]

Today, the stories about the spiritual and physical cures which occurred thanks to Ubald's healing masses are found not only in Rwanda but also in the West. There are testimonies of people in the United States such as Katsey in Jackson Hole in Wyoming who, for a long time was suffering from miscarriages but was healed and conceived a baby (as told by Cora Ligori) in 2011.[227] The daughter of Heidi Saxton in Chicago was healed from cancer in 2016;[228] Karen Brogan from Chicago attests that her little boy was healed from the rare rhabdomyosarcoma cancer.[229] As Ubald's travel schedule published online[230] shows, the priest-healer is requested in Africa and in the West, spending at least one week per month in the United States for healing prayers and animating sessions on the power of forgiveness and reconciliation. Ubald's healing ministry, followed by many stories, shows not only an African thirst for healing but a broad universal quest for healing even amidst the medically advanced nations. Ubald does not think he is the one who heals, but Christ through him. He does not think healing happens magically. He calls for human responsibility to participate in one's own and societal wellbeing.

---

[224] By "Our Lady of Kibeho" (officially called Our Lady of the Word) Fr. Ubald refers to the apparitions of Kibeho, Rwanda. According to Church officials and visionaries, our Lady of Kibeho appeared in Rwanda (1982-1989). Among visionaries, three ladies have been approved by the Church in 2006. Our Lady was calling Rwandans to conversion. It is said that the Virgin Mary alluded to the "river of blood" which was to flow in Rwanda if people do not convert and embrace love and sincere prayer. Many see this Marian message as a prophecy of genocide which occurred five years later after the cessation of apparitions in 1994. See http://www.kibeho-cana.org/a-brief-history-of-the-apparitions-of-our-lady-of-kibeho/

[225] See https://catholicherald.org/special-sections/mature-lifestyles/healing-comes-different-ways/

[226] Ibid.

[227] Fr. Ubald Rugirangoga, *Forgiveness Makes You Free*, 109.

[228] Ibid.

[229] Ibid, 101

[230] See https://frubald.com/about/travel-schedule/ accessed on March 28, 2019.

Within cultures marked by broken relationships within families, tribes, races, and nations, within medical and political structures, medicine and religion cannot attain their aim without compassion toward the most broken. Ubald calls us to cast our gaze to the wounded healer, Christ, who heals us from within and sets us free, when by his grace we follow his school of forgiveness and reconciliation. In Ubald's words "Jesus knows how evil touches our lives and causes us to suffer. We cannot choose whether we will suffer; we can only choose how we will respond to the suffering."[231] He adds "although it is Jesus who heals us, we must participate in our own healing. Do not blame others for not receiving the healing; it is not the fault of others. It is your responsibility, your opportunity, to receive healing. Even if others are praying for you, you must pray for yourself first. Others can help, but it is up to you."[232]

Nevertheless, the call for prayer and forgiveness as a path to healing is for us believers all-encompassing. It calls us to face ourselves with the eyes of God and appreciate the goodness within and beyond ourselves, and the grace bestowed in the created world, especially which helps us to care for ourselves and to care for others. In addition to restoring broken relationships between brothers and sisters, reconciliation calls for matching our religious faith in Christ the healer with our duty of being citizens, healers within our communities. While it is undeniable that many Africans die because of lack of adequate healing remedies, the possibility of faith-healing should not downplay recourse to natural remedies. The need is thus, in the language of Shawn Francis Peter, to reconcile sacred and secular responsibilities, our devotion to religion and our responsibility to selfcare and caring for others. [233]

OVERALL CONCLUDING REMARKS

The discussion we have held about African Catholic faith-healers and their surrounding motivations bring to light some major considerations:

First, faith-healing is not a one-person ministry. It involves the Church as a community of believers. It is at a large extent inspired by the encounter with Catholic Charismatic Renewal and practiced by clerical ministers in company with lay charismatic groups among the faithful. This has been observed in the case of Emmanuel Milingo in Zambia, Ubald Rugirangoga in Rwanda and Meinrad Hebga in Cameroun.

---

[231] Ibid. 114.
[232] Ibid. 115.
[233] See Shawn Francis Peter, *When Prayer Fails: Faith Healing, Children, and Law* (Oxford: Oxford University Press, 2008), 214.

Second, the people who come to faith-healers belong to various social strata, from rural and urban areas, from the poor and from the rich who encounter incurable ailments such as infertility, from both educated and from the uneducated persons. Although there are complicated health situations such as HIV-AIDS, cancers, infertility, and psychological trauma, we cannot hold that illnesses are not necessarily unpreventable and/or incurable in places where there are specialists and robust hospitals and dispensaries and various psycho-medical systems, and accessible mental health centers. While the Church in Africa already has health systems initiated by missionaries, there is a need is to improve them, and make efforts to bring affordable and accessible health systems to Africans.

Third, it would be unreasonable to impute whatever evils suffered by people in modern Africa to witchcraft and demonic or spiritual causes. Most diseases brought to faith-healers are psychosomatic and biological sicknesses, highly associated with social unrest, marriage breakdowns, stress resulting from overworking, anxiety caused by economic insecurity, unhealed physical and psychological wounds from crime such as genocide, fear of tribal and racial wars, poverty, illiteracy, destitution, and misery. Still the possibility of supernatural causes is not overlooked. Bernard Udelhoven presents an approach to the pastoral care of those who are afflicted by witchcraft.[234] He argues that the person who is seen as the victim of witchcraft become terrified and afflicted by lethargy that sometimes leads him/her to death. When the sick person is a Christian, we can suggest to him/her curative means accepted by Christianity. Witchcraft can be understood as a pathological state of believing in witchcraft assaults. It can be responded to by methods specific to religions, including Christians deprived of bishop-appointed exorcists. It could however be argued that religious practices performed during exorcism sessions seem narrower than their aim: healing. The aim is spiritual healing, an inner healing which can hopefully affect the whole person. It should not be only reduced to psychological remedies. It appeals to the faith of individuals who have a common understanding of illness and healing. Together the healer, the sick, and the supporting faithful share a vision of the world without which healing would be ineffective. Whether one believes in ancestral mindset, witchcraft, or demonic possession in the Christian sense, the cultural and spiritual pattern as well as the meaning given by the community are essential for understanding such types of illness and their remedies. In both cases, faith-healing may be a

---

[234] Bernhard Karl Udelhoven, *Unseen World: Dealing with Spirits, Witchcraft, and Satanism* (Lusaka, Zambia: FENZA, 2016), 405.

beneficial answer for those who are gifted and institutionally approved. As an essential aspect of the Gospel, healing is Christ's good news of the victory of life over death.

Fourth, one could appreciate; unlike Evangelical churches which tend to promote physical and spiritual healing, African Catholic healers who are rather discrete and somehow silent. Most of them know themselves as instruments of the healing power of Christ by witnessing the healing power of forgiveness and compassion, by administering sacraments and sacramentals such as holy water, through blessings, and through medical-traditional plants.

Fifth, many Catholic healers spontaneously describe different sorts of ailments suffered by the patients. Humility in talking about the results of the healings should be preserved and referring the patients to consult doctors needs to be emphasized. This could be an opportunity for modern medicine to extend *ad hoc* research on incurable and neglected diseases which often push the sick to look for faith-healers. It could also be an opportunity for experts in medicine, in psychology, and theology.[235]

Sixth, Meinrad Hebga's calls for a multidisciplinary approach in the ministry of healing stands out. For Hebga, spiritual healing cannot be efficient from the physical point of view.[236] While we could maintain the possibility of healing effected though prayer,[237] we should not fall into the danger of hypnotism or on the sensationalism which prevail among the therapists of the Independent Churches.

Seventh, there is a need for the universal Church and the African Catholic hierarchy to revisit African religion and its spiritual beliefs. African healing liturgies have been a point of disagreement especially with the Milingo case. Yet, as Terr Guerrie Har and other scholars acknowledge, healing through exorcism has always been an element of great solicitation from the Christian community in Africa and in the West.[238]

Lastly, faith-healing remains a subtle issue. It thus needs critical answers. My contentions have drawn from both skepticism and acceptance which surrounds this ministry in the Catholic Church. The matter remarkably has been discussed by magisterium in Africa and at the Vatican. In the case of Milingo, not only the Western missionaries, but also the Zambian local bishops were asking their

---

[235] G. C. Ikeobi, "Healing and Exorcism in Africa" S*piritus* 120 (1990), 246.
[236] M. P Hebga, *Sorcellerie: Chimère Dangereuse*? (Abidjan, Ivory Coast: Inades, 1979), 31.
[237] Ibid. 182.
[238] Guerrie Terr Haar, *Spirit of Africa. The Healing Ministry of Archbishop Milingo of Zambia* (London: C. Hurst & Co, 1992), 44.

archbishop to put an end to what he claimed to be a therapeutic experience. Milingo has been intensely accused of over-emphasizing the existence of the demon, of justifying the existence of most diseases by the influence of evil spirits, of imposing on Catholic Christianity the belief in the existence of an intermediary world between humans and God.[239] In the case of Fr. Hebga, Bishop Owono of Obala in Cameroon judged the healing ministry as dangerous and inappropriate for priests.[240] Yet in the Democratic Republic of Congo, Cardinal Malula authorized Fr. Alphonse Kabwila to practice this healing activity within his new school of prayer. His successor Cardinal Etsou did the same. Such a double authorization showed a clear openness of the African hierarchy to the question of the ministry of healing.[241] During the African Synod organized in Rome, the hierarchy issued an official point of view concerning these healing practices. Some bishops have spoken publicly in favor of the practice of the ministry of healing as a pastoral strategy for retaining Christians in the Church, as this practice may be a response to a more and more general need within the churches, in Christian communities in Africa. The Bishop of Congo Kinshasa, Nestor Ngoy declares: "in the face of the challenge that the sects are launching, we should re-evaluate the sacrament of the sick and the difficult and delicate ministry of exorcism which, alas, has not been retained "[242] As a whole, the African bishops say: "To help believers, it is necessary that we proclaim the power of Christ over all the spirits of evil, we need men and women who are holy and who, thanks to the sacrament and to the sacramentals and thanks to the prayers of healing, may come to help all those who are oppressed."[243] Yet the synodal final document did not pay attention to this demand.[244] One could see in this debate an invitation for a more discerning and enlightened Catholic bioethics, doctrinal and pastoral theology, as well as social and scientific approaches in matters of spiritual healing. This will be our concern in Chapter III.

---

[239] Ibid. 225-226.
[240] J. Owono, "Yes to the Ministry of Healing, No to Charlatanism" *Catholic Intellectuals*, 13 (1991), 14.
[241] Thomas, Louis Vincent, *Laissez Mon Peuple Aller! Eglise Africaine au-delà des Modèles?* (Paris: Karthala, 1987), 46.
[242] Ibid.
[243] Ibid.
[244] René Luneau, *Paroles and Silences du Synode Africain*, 1989-1995 (Paris: Karthala, 1997).

CHAPTER III

TOWARD AN EFFECTIVE FAITH-HEALING MINISTRY

In this last chapter, I would like to present a Catholic theological and pastoral approach as regards to faith-healing ministry. I begin by identifying the converging inspiration rooted Christianity and experiences lived in our time. The experience of faith-healing is an invitation for Africans to deepening the African culture with reason inspired by faith and sound ecclesial approaches of pastoral care of the sick and the needy.

3.1. THE CLAIM FOR HEALING MINISTRY

As we reflect on the ministry of faith healing, it is important to mention the claim for the healing by African believers. In addition to the challenges, we have mentioned in the previous chapters, different studies on African society reveal crucial problems that constitute an important issue for evangelization in Africa. Many specialists in health and religion, theologians, philosophers, sociologists, psychologists, anthropologists, historians as well as pastors and priests demonstrate not only the well-founded desire, but also and above all the need to address them. This understanding is supported by the experience of the Judeo-Christian faith where Christ performed and inspired the healing ministry.

To some extent, the ministry of Jesus, rooted in the Jewish culture, transpires within religious liturgies in Sub-Saharan Africa. Drawing from Benoit Awazi:

> In Black Africa as well as in the Old Testament, we are in the presence of a plethora of accounts of divine healing, exorcism, and the struggle between God and the evil spirits, the false gods (The Baals of the Old Testament). This pan-spiritualist and pan-religious vision of human destiny gives serious and solid reasons for the socio-political and cultural deployment of healing and liberation-based theologians on the divine healing by faith and the exorcisms which logically ensue. [245]

In the African healing ministry, a special reference to Jesus' commission to the disciples is cherished: "cure the sick, raise the dead, cleanse the lepers, cast out demons. You received without payment, give without payment" (Mt 10:8). This text emphasizes the practice of exorcisms and healing as one

---

[245] Benoit Awazi Mbambi Kungua, *Panorama des Théologies Négro-Africaines* (Paris: L'Harmattan, 2002), 91.

spiritual ministry. An observation of the practices of exorcism and healing in Africa reveals the same conviction. Yet what we need to highlight here is exorcisms carried out by those mandated by the Church in accordance with Canon 1172; the lay ministers and/or priests who carry out public healing masses and other forms of prayer for healing. During sessions of exorcisms, physical healing is sometimes observed, and during healing prayers for the sick. There are many cases of exorcisms. Some examples could be found in the healing prayers organized by parish priests with the approval of bishops in the African megacities and certain rural centers such as at Lagos in Nigeria, at Johannesburg in South-Africa, in Nairobi, Kenya at the Thika Vincentian Retreat Center. Rwanda alone has many: at Kigali National Stadium and in the surrounding cities such as in the South-West of Rwanda at Rusizi, with Catholic Healing Center such as the Centre of the Secret of Peace,[246] in southern Rwanda at Ruhango where monthly healing prayers are organized at the Catholic Center of the Merciful-Jesus.[247] The Democratic Republic of Congo (D.R.C) did not stay without healers, in the capital city of Kinshasa and in most provincial capitals where big gatherings of the Charismatic Renewal are held, in Kindu, Bukavu and Goma. Cameroon knows many traditional and Christian healers at Yaoundé and Douala. In Bujumbura in Burundi and in Lusaka in Zambia Catholic healers are well documented. The healing prayers bring together members of the Church from different countries (Uganda, Cameroon, Benin, Togo, Italy, D.R.C) where accounts of exorcisms and physical healing are remarkably numerous. Prayers of exorcism are also held in various parishes, where physical healing are experienced by people suffering from chronic headaches, ulcers, stomach pains, and hypertension crises, as well as testimonies of healing from the attacks of malevolent forces.

Our discernment of exorcism and healing calls us to have in mind possible signs of evil possession. Experts in the field, such as Dom Gabriel Amorth, a former renowned exorcist at the Vatican, as well as Mgr. Tournyol du Clos, agree on four groups of different forms of evil possessions.[248]

3.1.1. DIABOLIC POSSESSION: Where the demon acts in the patient's body, he takes possession of the body of a person or causes him to act or speak

---

[246] https://frubald.com/the-center-for-the-secret-of-peace/ Accessed on March 30th, 2019.

[247] https://www.sanctuaireruhango.info, Accessed on March 31, 2019.

[248] Dom Gabriel Amorth, *Un Exorciste Raconte* (Paris: Edition du Rocher, 2010), 41. See also Mgr. Tournyol du Clos, *Le Combat Avancé de l'Eglise* (Canohès, France: L'Archistratège, 2012), 138.

under his control, without the victim being able to resist him. It is in this case that paranormal phenomena such as "speaking unknown languages and understanding them, revealing distant and hidden facts, making use of extraordinary force, having a virulent aversion to God, Jesus, the Virgin Mary, the Sacraments, manifesting a cold, cruel selfishness or a conscious and fierce fear."[249] These signs show demonic possession which can be healed by exorcism.

3.1.2. EVIL VEXATION. By this the demon can cause disorders in health, in material goods, in human affections, in one's work. It can be manifest in diseases refractory to medical treatment, affective crises of husbands with their wives at night. Dom Gabriel Amorth interprets the experience of Saint Paul as a case of diabolical vexation of a malefic order:[250] "Therefore, to keep me from being elated, a thorn was given to me in the flesh, a messenger of Satan to torment me in the flesh, to keep me from being elated "(2 Cor 12:7).

3.1.3. DIABOLICAL OBSESSION. A series of temptations more violent and more prolonged than ordinary temptations. One experiences obsessive thoughts, absurd, even blasphemous, difficult, and sometimes impossible to free oneself. Some even lead to suicide.

Fourth, *diabolical infestation*: the devilish attack on different objects, houses, animals, as is illustrated in the Gospels (Mk 5:11-13).

3.1.4. HOSTILITY TOWARDS DIVINE VALUES. Other secondary cases of diabolical influence are mentioned, as such hostility about divine values, hate of the sacred, religious doubt, the incapacity to experience a real contrition of sin, the impossibility to concentrate for prayer and for the reading of Holy Scripture, anguish, irritability, aggression, kleptomania, drug addiction, etc. These are doorways and signs for diabolical influences.

Surprising though it may seem, the Devil could bring one to the knowledge of God, to be converted, to even a deeper spiritual life. John Chrysostom preached the Devil as an instrument of sanctification, certainly not to attribute to it the merit, but to glorify the wisdom of God who makes everything serve our good, (Rom 8:28). Dismantling the governance of the world by demons, in his Homilies, St John Chrysostom states:

---

[249] Michel Dubost, Stanislas Lalane, eds. *Le Nouveau Théo, Encyclopédie Catholique pour Tous* (Paris: Mane, Michel, 2019), 685.

[250] Dom Gabriel Amorth, *Un Exorciste Raconte*, 42.

The Devil then is acknowledged, as I said, to be evil by all. What shall we say about this beautiful and wondrous creation? (...). For it is not wicked but is both beautiful and a token of the wisdom and power and lovingkindness of God (...). The Devil is nowhere here, but the creation alone is set before us as the teacher of the knowledge of God."[251] He adds, "certain demon-possessed men met Jesus as they were coming out of some tombs and the demons beseeched him to let them go into a herd of pigs, and he let them go, and they went away immediately and threw themselves over a cliff. (...). What incurable damage would they have devised. For this reason, that you may learn about their wickedness in the bodies of the irrational creatures (...). And so now when you see someone disturbed by a demon, worship your Master, learn of demon wickedness. For it is possible to learn of both these in cases of these demon-possessed men, both God's benevolence and the demon's evil.[252]

Exorcism and healing could be sometimes an opportunity for conversion, a profound integration and a return to the Catholic faith. In addition to this conversion, there are others which resist malefic attacks such as prayer, sacraments, charity, forgiveness, recourse to Marian devotion, saints, and angels, and so on.

Meinrad Hebga has advocated for a pastoral care of intelligence, of moral discernment rooted in the intellectual capacities, avoiding the propagandist tendency, triumphalism and proselytism, mercantilism, and ignorance. The concern for healing should attract our attention in the Church to avoid exposing our faithful Catholics and other believers to the mercy of gurus, who cleverly exploit and manipulate people's consciences.[253]

To achieve this, R. de Haes[254] recommends we examine all these problems through a holistic and eschatological lens. Buetubela Balembo[255] deplores the fact that the problems of diseases, witchcraft, and possession are the great ones absent from our theological curricula and even theological reflection. One would rightly add that these questions are not strictly speaking

---

[251] St. John Chrysostom's Homilies, See https://www.roger-pearse.com/weblog/wp-content/uploads/2014/05/chrysostom-devil-bryson-2014.pdf. Accessed on March 31, 2019.
[252] Ibid.
[253] Meinrad Hebga as cited by Nestor Salumu Ndalibandu, *Les Prières d'Exorcismes et de Guérison dans l'Eglise Catholique en Afrique* (Paris, L'Harmatan, 2017), 58.
[254] R. Haes as cited by Nestor Salumu Ndalibandu, *Les Prières d'Exorcismes et de Guérison dans l'Eglise Catholique en Afrique*, 58.
[255] Buetubela Balembo as cited by Nestor Salumu Ndalibandu, *Les Prières d'Exorcismes et de Guérison dans l'Eglise Catholique en Afrique*, 58.

part of the teaching program in the major seminary in terms of initiation of the current and future priests.

With Stan Chu Ilo and Bernhard Udelhoven's *Unseen World*,[256] looking at the suffering peoples who seek miraculous healing through Eucharistic celebrations, through faith-healing crusades in Africa, the people who run miles into deserted places and visit water pools as Odomiri Bethsaida,[257] considering their thirst for a possible divine healing, we contend that the solution does not rely in theological skepticism which considers faith-healing as an enchantment and take it as irrelevant in every way. Still, we are not to reduce medical care to faith-healing (the danger of Evangelical movements and extreme Catholic charismatic renewal). We need to search for healing within a broader perspective and so propose a comprehensive approach which does justice to the very inception of health and wholeness as spiritual and physical, as social and moral.

We are quite convinced that thousands of people who attend Ubald Rugirangoga's healing masses in Rwanda, that the believers and non-believers who go to the Vincentian Healing Retreat at Thika in Nairobi,[258] those who frequent Odomiri Bethsaida's pool in Nigeria, people who go to fetch healing waters at Kibeho Marian Shrine in Rwanda and those who attend different crusades of prayer, crossing miles in the search for healing in many parts of Africa, reveal our profound wounded humanity in their bodies and in their soul. They call us to follow Christ, the wounded healer, the Lord who invites us to diligently love and serve the poor, to accompany and care for the sick, the disabled, and the broken-hearted among us. Discernibly, we all need God's healing, for we are sinners, spiritually and physically limited in one way or another. Yet God's effective healing works through his grace and our agency in the world. The search for miraculous healing should not be the *telos*, our end is to be liberated, saved, our end is a beatific vision with God, when God will be all in all (1 Cor 15:28), a journey which starts here and now.

That said, the people who look for the miraculous healing to a large extent are not repulsed by medical systems. They do not find adequate and accessible

---

[256] See Bernhard Udelhoven, *Unseen World: Dealing with Spirits, Witchcraft, and Satanism* (Lusaka, Zambia: FENZA, 2015).
[257] See Stan Chu Ilo, *Wealth, Health, and Hope in African Christian Religion* (Lanham, MD: Lexington, 2018), 45.
[258] See http://www.vrcthika.org. Vincentian Retreat Center in Nairobi Kenya is run by priest of Vincentian Congregation. As the website describes, the sick and suffering, the broken-hearted, the poor, the needy who come to the center continue to witness the divine intervention in their lives through wonderous miracles in the form of conversion, healing from sickness, deliverance and from different forms of addictions.

healing systems, either in the traditional or modern medicine. Called to love and serve in the world, the Church in Africa ought to discern what should be done from the perspective of our faith and Church teachings to addressing this suffering. How does Catholic bio-ethics help for an effective faith-healing in Africa? A faith-healing ministry that genuinely values health and wholeness, in addition to prayer and liturgical devotions, needs to consider that Catholic faith is richly equipped with resources that could effectively promote health for the Sub-Saharan Africans.

3.2. Criteria of Discernment

Without a pretention to exhaust our rich Catholic resources and to solve all problems, we argue in the following section that faith-healing could be effective by discerning: 1) The Preferential Option for The Poor, 2) The Art of Accompaniment, 3) The Multi-secterial and Bio-social Approach, 4) The Doctrinal and Pastoral Approach.

3.2.1. The Preferential Option for The Poor.
"There will always be poor in the land. Therefore, I command you to be open handed toward your fellows...who are poor and needy in your land." (Dt 15:10-11)

The principle of the preferential option for the poor encourages actions toward those most affected in need, including those who are sick. Lisa Cahill's work, "AIDS, Justice and The Common Good" highlights the preferential option for the poor as "a duty of human justice and of Christian love."[259] In the view of Pope John Paul II, the preferential option for the poor has a biblical value. In his several instances, the Pontiff called for solidarity with most victims of social problems. He noted, "It is above all the poor to whom Jesus speaks in his preaching and actions."[260] Evidently the preferential option for the poor guides our commitments to where people suffer most from health inequalities, poverty, and diseases.

This said, we do not reduce the poor to poverty; Sub-Saharan Africa is not the poorest area in the world. It is, on the contrary, gifted with a natural heritage,

---

[259] Lisa Cahill, "Aids, Justice and the Common Good" in *Catholic Ethicists on HIV/AIDS Prevention.* ed. J. F. Keenan (New York: Continuum, 2000), 289.
[260] Pope John Paul II, *Gospel of Life* as cited by Lisa Cahill in « Aids, Justice and the Common Good » 289.

with minerals, the fauna and flora, pristine tropical forests which harbor varieties of traditional medicinal herbs, inhabited by sage elderly and with a large part of a lively and creative youth generation, where the tradition and modernity meet and flourish.

As Jon Sobrino rightly noted, "poverty is an historical fact". While we do not ignore the reality of inherent moral evil of our fallen humanity, we have to emphasize that poverty as a medium culture of diseases in Africa is rooted in structural violence. "The poor are "impoverished"[261] hence, *diseased.* Poverty can be resisted, reduced, and diseases can be treated and healed. As Sobrino laments,

> Poverty (…) is the most lasting form of violence and the violence that is committed with the greatest impunity. Holocausts and Massacres-sometimes produce their Nuremberg but not…the exploitation of Africa. What court of appeal is there for the thirty-five or forty million people who die annually of hunger-related diseases. And the most maddening thing is that today it is possible to eliminate poverty.[262]

What Jon Sobrino said eighteen years ago remains a reality today. According to the reports of experts, extreme poverty has been declining worldwide. The World Bank's Report estimates that the number of people living in extreme poverty (below US$1.90 per day) has fallen from 1.9 billion in 1990 to about 736 million in 2015.[263] Yet extreme poverty continues to escalate in sub-Saharan Africa, which counted in 2015 more than half of the world's population surviving on less than US$1.90 per day. Statistics indicate that this region will count in 2050 almost 90% of people living in extreme poverty.[264] Extreme poverty literally kills. Hunger, malnutrition, and diseases claim the lives of millions each year. Poverty stricken states tend to have weak institutions and are plagued by ineffective governance, rendering them unable to meet their basic needs for food, sanitation, health care, and education.

Agnes Binagwaho et al. in *The Lancet,* while recognizing the progress in the life expectancy in many countries of Africa, see prevalent health problems in Sub-Saharan Africa. For them, Sub-Saharan Africa faces a double burden of traditional and persisting health challenges, such as infectious diseases, malnutrition, child and maternal disability, emerging challenges resulting from

---

[261] Jon Sobrino, *Christ The Liberator* (Maryknoll, NY: Orbis, 2001), 4.
[262] Ibid., 5.
[263] https://openknowledge.worldbank.org/bitstream/handle/10986/30418/9781464813066_Ch01.pdf, 21. Accessed on 30 March, 2019.
[264] Ibid.

an escalating prevalence of chronic conditions, mental health disorders, injuries, health problems associated with environmental degradation and climate change.[265]

Pope Francis, the prophet of the preferential option for the poor today, is right to compare Africa as such to a man in the parable of Luke, who, while travelling from Jerusalem to Jericho, "fell into the hands of robbers who stripped him, beat him and went away, leaving him half dead" (Lk 10: 31-32).[266]

The preferential option for the poor involves overcoming the temptation of money, pride and prestige. Emmanuel Milingo denounced this temptation as following:

> As we carry out the work of deliverance, we must be aware of our instrumentality. Any speck of pride in our attitude towards the possessed, any hint of pride in our words, will weaken the power in us to carry out duty to deliver our brothers and sisters from the evil spirits. To avoid all these human elements in this special work we need to become permanent habitations of the Holy Spirit.[267]

It is said that money is a two-edged sword, a good master but a bad servant. 1 Tim 6:10 suggests that money is the root of all evil. This is not to condemn the search and the use of money, but to call for discipleship prudence in searching it and in using it. Money is not the only reward a disciple-healer may receive as an exchange of the service he/she has performed. Many faith-healers are respected due to the precious gift they have received. They may receive important prestige in form of social rewards. Although rewarding healers may happen, there are rewards which may compromise the demands of discipleship. A faith-healer could be respected for her/her compassion, for his/her spirituality in helping sick persons, and could easily be seen as a model of discipleship. Jesus has boldly said to his apostles: "cure the sick, raise the dead, cleanse the lepers, cast out the demons, you received without payment; give without payment," (Mt 10:8). The apostles were to live from the material support on the behalf of the people to whom they were ministering. They were not supposed to receive material reward for healing. The disciples were not supposed to request money because of performing miracles. The same invitation of Jesus to healers remains, as one doctor reminded Milingo: "I strongly advise

---

[265] Agnes Binagwaho https://www.thelancet.com/journals/lancet/article/PIIS0140-6736(17)31509-X/fulltext. Accessed on March 30, 2019.

[266] See https://cruxnow.com/global-church/2018/06/23/africa-needs-christian-unity-to-survive-being-half-dead-pope-says/ accessed on March 31, 2019.

[267] Ibid, 60.

you not to charge patients... to receive remuneration."[268] One renowned Catholic priest-healer is Fr. McAlear. As a Catholic Newsletter reports of him, McAlear receives no fee for his visit and depends entirely on offerings for his travel expenses. McAlear does not claim to have the gift of healing, but only the gift of prayer. In his words: "We pray to God, and this happens, I know it is not me. I know God is there and I'm almost watching him do things, it is Jesus' compassion, the love of God that is doing healing."[269] Any greed toward money could be seen to be contrary to the manners of proceeding of the Holy Spirit. The book of Acts exemplifies the extent to which the Apostles were called to categorically refuse any money as reward for their prayer service. The Samaritan great man called Simon who used to practice magic in the city was tempted to give money to Peter for laying hands on him as a reward of being given the Holy Spirit. Peter firmly rebuked him saying "May your silver perish with you, because you thought you could gain God's gift with money! You have no part or share in this for your heart is not right before God." (Acts 8:22). As with the early apostles, healing should not be performed for gain in the Church. The apostle Peter who received the gift of healing summons the elders of the faithful, to 'tend the flock of God'... 'exercising the oversight, not under compulsion but willingly...not for sordid gain but eagerly...not lord it over but be examples to the flock' for God opposes the proud but gives grace to the humble" (1 Peter 5: 1-5).

A response to the desperation and ill-health of impoverished Sub-Saharan Africans, of the frustrated young people, of the lament and pain of the elderly, or of the wounds of survivors of genocides, democides, war crimes, and human rights violations lies in the proclamation of the Gospel to the poor. It implies devoting "attention to creating a Christian *habitus*, spirit-led dispositions that will guide the actions of individuals and communities."[270] It calls for translating the word of God and Christian liturgies into experiences of hopes, love, joy, and harmony. In this perspective, Sub-Saharan Africa would become a haven of the healing hand of Christ. As Nestor Salumu Ndalibandu suggests, this will see the day by tapping into local, cultural, and material resources;[271] by addressing inequities and inequalities that devastate our society. The duty of the Church is clear: to foster efforts, to promote a wise and ethical management of the African natural heritage and resources.

---

[268] Ibid., 20.
[269] See http://www.frmac.org/testimonials.html. Accessed on December 11, 2018.
[270] Robert Ewusie *Moses, Practices of Power*, 232.
[271] Nestor, Salumu Ndalibandu, *Les Prieres d'Exorcisme et de Guerison dans l'Eglise Catholique en Afrique*, 64.

The preferential option for the poor is the mission that Jesus gave to the young man as he says, "go and sell everything you have and give it to the poor" (Lk 18: 22). It entails both restorative and distributive justice. It ought to be rooted in an active compassion toward the last and the least, the broken-hearted ones, the survivors of human-made and natural evils, including the sick and the devil-attacked ones, those obsessed by what debilitates well-being. It calls us to reach out to those in need of justice and peace in the peripheral areas of conflicts, into aggressive families and inimical communities; it invites us to solidary efforts as one and entire mystical body of Christ that strives for the common good, that defends human dignity, that seeks the freedom and rights of each and all men and women, to accompanying each and all in need.

3.2.2. THE ART OF ACCOMPANIMENT. "Plans are established by seeking advice, so if you wage a war, obtain guidance" (Pr. 20: 18).

The art of accompaniment seeks to identify the hidden wounds of those who are seeking God for health, wealth, and healing. The art of accompaniment requires Church ministers, priests, and theologians to reach out to people who are looking for a "miraculous stream" such in Nigeria,[272] those who seek the wilderness of the pristine forests in Sub-Saharan Africa, as well as those who are looking for Jesus-the-healer in the sanctuaries of the Merciful-Jesus in Rwanda. Today's advocate of accompaniment is Pope Francis.

The successor of St. Peter invites us to the art of accompaniment which implies "removing our sandals" to meet our brothers and sisters in need. They are indeed a sacred humanity which cries out for our spiritual and pastoral proximity. Pope Francis put it: "no matter how weak or vulnerable, we must remember that we are standing on holy ground."[273] The art of accompaniment calls for humility, honesty, for a *metanoia*, an openness of heart and a genuine spiritual encounter.[274] Accompaniment as a pastoral presence is rooted in the incarnation of Christ, a total identification with humanity, especially with the people in need, sharing their experiences, their vulnerabilities, their struggles, and their hopes.

---

[272] See Stan Chu Ilo "Searching for Healing in a Miraculous Stream: The fate of God's People in Africa" *Wealth, Health, and Hope in African Christian Religion*. Lanham—London: Lenxington Books), 45.

[273] Pope Francis cited in Stan Chu Ilo "The Church of Pope Francis: An Ecclesiology of Accountability," *The Church We Want: African Catholics Look to Vatican II,* ed. A. E. Orobator (Maryknoll, NY: Orbis Books, 2016), 26.

[274] Chu Ilo, "Searching for Healing in a Miraculous Stream," 74.

In his speech to newly appointed bishops on September 19, 2013, Pope Francis stresses that the art of accompaniment requires pastoral presence which requires us to become pastors who have "the smell of the sheep" because the ministers are amid the people like Jesus was with his disciples.[275] Pope Francis invites us to enter the life of the poor and take journey with them. It entails being present where the poor are living. It invites us to pay attention to stories of the survivors of genocides and millions of people affected by insecurities and civil wars in Rwanda and Burundi, it entails reaching out to refugees and displaced people of Eastern Democratic Republic of Congo, to listen to the unheard laments of childless families, the moans of orphans, the cries of the widows and widowers. We are to go where numbers of people are mentally wounded by the hatred, by violence, and tribal killings, to the ones anguished by the lack of unemployment, others enduring family breakdowns, others spiritually devastated by family breakups, and others suffering from permanent repressive political regimes. Within such miscellaneous psychological and physical threats, spiritual attacks may not miss weak entries, while bodily vulnerabilities find a fertile ground. This is a call to discipleship of accompaniment. For Pope Francis, accompaniment is not a reserve of priests or pastors. It encompasses the Church's ministers and lay Christians, and whoever is touched by God's love in our churches and moved to make a home for all, especially with and for the poor. [276] More than being a service or a ministry, accompaniment is a vocation of living with the poor and being hospitable to them.

> Accompaniment signifies openness to others especially those on the margins in places where they feel pain and empty, or where they are crying for help. Accompaniment viewed in this light is a relationship characterized by the same qualities which are reflected in the mutual indwelling or hospitality at the heart of Trinitarian life. The three divine persons make room for each other. Thus, to accompany someone is to dwell in common with that person in relationship of mutuality and respect. It requires an openness to be with another especially in their places and sites of pain because people see God's presence in each other no matter what their social status and economic or spiritual circumstances.[277]

---

[275] Pope Francis, *The Church of Mercy: A Vision for the Church* (Chicago: Loyola Press, 2014), 77.

[276] Stan Chu Ilo, "Searching for Healing in a Miraculous Stream," 74.

[277] See Janice Price, *World Shaped Mission: Reimagining Mission Today* (London: Church House

This art of accompaniment strongly fits into the African communitarian ethic, by which all things and people are interconnected by "a vital union of mutual participation in the life of all."[278] The reflection made by Placide Tempels about Bantu in Black Africa confirms the inescapable role of community as a means in search of healing. According to Tempels, "the Bantu cannot conceive ... the human person as an independent being standing on his own. Every human person, every individual is as it were one link in a chain of vital forces: a living link both exercising and receiving influences, a link that establishes the bond with previous generations and with the forces that support his own existence."[279]

Communitarian accompaniment acknowledges that one's suffering is the suffering of the whole community. The sickness that affects my neighbor is my sickness, and the cry of the earth is my cry. The African community paradigm acknowledges that everyone is concerned with the reality of suffering. In other words, everyone is called to participate in bringing about healing to his or her neighbor and to the whole community. This participative accompaniment constitutes a vital union which brings harmony as "everyone works and walks together for justice to reign on earth."[280]

Participative accompaniment as an instrument of personal and community healing cannot be achieved without what Samuel Pobee in reference to Greek, calls *metanoia*. Pobee emphasizes *metanoia* in the context of the search for religious human rights in Africa, which rights once violated, affect the totality of the human person, including one's enjoyment of integral health. Pobee's proposition is also helpful in the search for healing and health in Africa. As Pobee noted, *metanoia* or repentance is the remedy of human propensity to sin, sins of commission, sins of omission, the acts of denying love of God and of neighbor. The basic meaning of *metanoia* is change of mind. *Metanoia* has a very profound ethical significance. It denotes the fact of feeling sorry, changing one's mind and doing acts of expiation for wrongs committed, calling for a radical change in relation to God, to humanity, and to creation as a whole. As Fr. Ubald would agree, *metanoia* precedes spiritual and physical healing when one recognizes her/his past errors, confesses his/her guilt; asks for forgiveness, and repents.

2012), 24.
[278] Stan Chu Ilo, "Searching for Healing in a Miraculous Stream," 75.
[279] Placide Tempels quoted in Bénézet Bujo, *Foundations of An African Ethic* (Freiburg: Crossroad Publishing Company, 2016), 86.
[280] Ibid.

As Pope Francis noted, to accompany others is to dare to face the mystery of God's presence in the life of another person. Hence, we ought to listen carefully to how God calls each person.[281] Hence, the art of accompaniment, beyond being a mere hearing, ought to learn the art of listening. "To listen is to have an open heart," that guides to a sincere encounter and "intimacy with Christ."[282]

3.3.3. A MULTI-SECTORIAL AND BIO-ETHICAL PERSPECTIVE: "God heals the brokenhearted, binding up their injuries" (Ps 147:3)

Attention must be given to a theological bioethical approach aiming at detecting real cases of either spiritual or physical influence in people who ask for care. As a point of departure, this needs an appreciation of the positive values in African cultures that can be useful and relevant in this healing ministry. Sub-Saharan Africans have been rightly or wrongly criticized for a certain syncretism, perhaps mainly of their deep religious attachment of the ancestors and belief in spirits which communicate with God and related practices found in many religious cultures. As John Samuel Pobee[283] and Laurenti Magesa[284] have argued, atheism is utterly absent in Sub-Saharan Africa. Yet as Benoit Awazi has pointed out, apart from the Supreme God-infused people, the life of Sub-Saharan Africans is also conditioned by "the perverse and idolatrous practices of witchcraft, bewitching, spells, and dark magic (ancestral fears) that are legion in Africa."[285] Nestor Salumu admits,

Many Sub-Saharan Africans explain the events not necessarily with the rational categories of Western inspiration in which their pastors were formed, but also and especially by the recourse to the metaphysical causes, to the symbolic and narrative language (dreams, myths, dreams) recites, proverbs, rites, dances, songs, spirits, good and bad, diviners.[286]

---

[281] *The Joy of the Gospel*, 171.
[282] Bill Huerbsch, *The Art of Accompaniment* (New London, CT: Twenty-Third Publications, 2017), 14.
[283] See Samuel Pobee, "Africa's Search for Religious Human Rights Through Returning to Wells of Living Water," *Religious Human Rights in Global Perspective: Legal Perspectives*. ed. Johan D.van der Vyer and John Witte, Jr. (The Hague--London: Martinus Nijhoff, 1996), 392.
[284] Laurenti Magesa, *African Religion: The Moral Tradition of Abundant life* (Maryknoll, NY : Orbis, 1997), 6.
[285] Benoit Awazi Mbambi Kungua, *Panorama of Anglophone Negro-African Theologies*, 95.
[286] Nestor Salumu Ndalibandu, *Les Prières d'Exorcismes et de Guérison dans l'Eglise Catholique en Afrique* (Paris: L'Harmattan), 62.

These conceptions are often experienced in the forms of popular religiosity in Africa. Among believers, the local name of the God we believe in in Christianity is the same as one of the ancestors. The Banyarwanda will call God, Imana; the Barundi, Mungu; Ngai among the Kikuyu of Kenya, and Katonda in the Baganda of Uganda. The same names which were used in the traditional African religions are preserved to name the God taught by Christianity. One would wonder if there has been a deeper epistemological shift that may help the Sub-Saharan Africans approach or better conceive God as triune, as a God of love and compassion, not only a transcendent, almighty God, but God-Immanuel, God with and for us. As Benoit Awazi contends, the time is ripe for African scholarship to review the traditions that crystallize the fear of witchcraft, the psychosis of spirits and divination practices that can endanger any process of various attacks against the diabolical influence in all its forms. [287]

Within various African cultures where the religious factor is the main guide to the reading of the real and the events of life, it is necessary to consider this cultural specificity of African societies in the search for practical and contextual solutions to the problems related to witchcraft. Given the pervasiveness of Evangelical Christian churches and Catholic Charismatic Renewal, with their theology of exorcism and the constant quest for divine healing, the time is ripe for the Church in Africa to incarnate a proper and effective pastoral care that eradicates sorcery in the daily practices of Africans.[288]

The invitation here is the need for critical studies of cultural identities within which to place these health threats of witches and crises of divination, as well as critical studies of those who are suffering from ordinary diseases. Drawing from Gilbert Shimba[289]: "Our faith as Africans is still enveloped in a culture not entirely evangelized."[290] Thus "African priests who pray for the sick persons, in addition to the knowledge of psychology, of anthropology, of sociology and theology, have to consider culture, or the transgression of certain taboos, and an imbalance that affects what constitutes social relations."[291]

---

[287] Benoit Awazi Bambi Kungua, *De la Post-Colonie à la Mondialisation Néolibérale : Radioscopie Ethique de la Crise Négro-Africaine* (Paris: L'Harmattan, 2011), 67.

[288] Ibid.

[289] Shimba Banza is an African theologian from the Democratic Republic of Congo ; his publications include *Initiation à la Théologie Africaine* (Paris: Edilivre, 2012), and Comment Guérir par La Prière (Kinshasa, Democratic Republic of Congo: Médiaspaul, 2005).

[290] Gilbert Shimba Ganza, *Comment Guérir par La Prière*, 12.

[291] Ibid.

In the same conviction, Meinrad Hebga calls for instituting a substantiated theology that deals with inherent questions to manage the issues of disease and healing in Sub-Saharan Africa. In his words: "It is therefore time to put a *diakonia* of culture-related diseases. Let us not refrain in a scientific verbalism without consistency, in the name of psychoanalysis or the demythization of evangelizers"[292]

Suffering and sickness always have a negative consideration that could make the faithful enemies of the cross and reject a positive dimension of the way to Christ so that the cross becomes the bedrock of glory. For many Africans, all suffering, illness, and even death always have a cause. Yet the quest for miracles in divine healing must in no way become an end. It must in no way renounce and escape at once the decisive test of the cross, which alone decides in the last instance the Christianity of a theology. It must not lead to the flight of the daily cross and to the paths of ease mirrored to Jesus by the tempter in the desert. [293]

The response to the demands of our daily crosses can be found in our traditional and cultural values where exorcism and healing ministry could contribute to addressing the prevailing suffering of Africans. Within this quandary a double trend is observed. One which demeans the demon and denies its existence, explaining the phenomena of possession or others as facts qualified as psychological crisis and of purely spiritual origin. The other trend sees the demon everywhere and makes it even responsible for all the problems that occur in society. This situation sometimes unfortunately justifies a certain indifference of the Church leadership to exorcism and healing. As Patrizia Cattaneo observes, "It is the notorious technique of the evil one who, to make believe a lie ... the final goal is to break the unicity of the Church."[294]

To address these deviations in healing ministry, Benoit Awazi upholds Meinrad Hebga's recommendation which calls for an urgent, fruitful, and critical dialogue. The latter must be made by African theologians inspired by values found in the African Traditional Religions.[295] Hebga invites for a healing and liberating theology based on faith-healing, still welcoming the contributions of other disciplines such as sociology, psychology, anthropology, and

---

[292] M. P. Hebga, *Le Ministère de Guérison : Monopole des Sectes et Églises Indépendantes*, 1993-1994, ..., 419.

[293] Ibid.

[294] Patrizia Cattaneo as cited by Nestor Salumu Ndalibandu, *Les Prières d'Exorcismes et de Guérison dans l'Eglise Catholique en Afrique*, 65.

[295] Benoit Awazi Mbambi, *Panorama de la Théologie Négro-Africaine Contemporaine*, 77.

philosophy. To do this, the Catholic orthopraxis and orthodoxy must prevail, in discerning the elements compatible with the Gospel from those which are incompatible, to enhance the culture of integral liberation, to enhance not just health but also salvation of each and all peoples. Pope Benedict XVI encourages the indispensable need of discernment enlightened by faith and reason to avoid vicious consequences.[296] Stan Chu Ilo argues that African theologies, sociologies, religious studies, medicine, not-for-profit research, and advocacy seek diverse and converging approaches regarding health and healing in Africa.[297] Chu Ilo draws from Bernhard Udelhoven who calls for a multidisciplinary framework in matters of spiritual healing. Such a comprehensive approach, also understood as a biosocial approach, has lately been advocated by Paul Farmer, Eugene T. Richardson, Mohammed Bailor, J. Daniel Kelly, Yusupha Dibba, and Songor Koedoyoma in their fight against diseases such as Ebola epidemic on the African continent.[298] Yet, it would be incomplete to look only at the social and biological causes of diseases, while overlooking their spiritual causes. We thus need a wider embracing approach which Stan Chu Ilo proposes as a biosocial theological approach.

For Stan Chu Ilo, a biosocial theological approach relates the problems of poverty and susceptibility of diseases. As Paul Farmer noted, there is a "preferential option" which diseases make on the poor. The poor are the most affected by diseases. A biosocial theological approach seeks to disrupt "multiple frames of reference with regard to health care about lifestyles, social conditions of people, economic status, disability, and how they all impact health" [299] A biosocial theological approach draws insight from McKeown's research.

According to McKeown, the decline of mortality and illnesses in England and Wales in the nineteenth and twentieth centuries was not a result of a merely medical intervention but "owed a good deal to medical measures as it has been influenced by general improvements in the standard of living, particularly in respect to infant feeding and care."[300]

Despite some disagreement with McKeown's thesis about how we would track improvements through public health and therapeutic medicine, many

---

[296] Pope Benedict XVI as cited in *Les Prières d'Exorcismes et de Guérison dans l'Eglise Catholique en Afrique*, 66.
[297] Stan Chu Ilo, "Searching for Healing in A Miraculous Stream," 55.
[298] See Paul Farmer, et al. "Biosocial Approaches to the 2013-2016 Ebola Pandemic" *Health and Human Rights Journal*, vol.18,1 (2016), 117.
[299] Paul Farmer, et al., *Reimagining Global Health: An Introduction* (Berkeley, CA: University of California Press, 2013), 7.
[300] See Thomas McKeown quoted by Stan Chu Ilo "Searching for Healing in a Miraculous Stream", 56.

would agree that improved social environmental, and economic conditions, together with accessible and adequate medical care are responsible for the decline in the mortality rate in UK and in Western countries in general. Thus, McKeown suggests that health interventions such as vaccination, modern and well-equipped hospitals, healing pastors and healing homes, distribution of mosquito nets, and medical doctors are "good in themselves." These conditions, however, would not guarantee the health of people if their conditions of life are not improved. [301]

What the authors propose, health and healing in Africa needs an integrated multi-secterial approach, involving diverse levels of commitment. Africans should not see sickness as a matter of solely spiritual causes which will be healed by faith healers, nor by limiting or reducing diseases of biological causes which can be addressed by medical doctors. Drawing from James Cochrane, Chu Ilo proposes the model of the African Religious Health Assets Program (ARHAP) which has started developing a biosocial theological approach. ARHAP sees "health and healing as a convergence of multiple ways of seeing the world which must take stock of inherited or socialized knowledge about health and wellbeing for an effective and sustainable intervention."[302]

As Chu Ilo highlights, the biosocial theological approach sees sickness, health, and healing as a way of upholding human and cosmic life by bringing together all realities which contribute to the procurement of abundant life, especially in the face of sickness and death. Chu Ilo's views are upheld by Davison Telen Banda. In Banda's view, a Jesus Christ who is narrowly concerned with eschatological life while neglecting the wholeness of life, including well-being is not welcome in Africa. As Banda put it, "The Jesus for Africa should always transcend the emotional crisis of the moment. He should transform life beyond the revival rally, to continue as the believer faces daunting questions of trusting in all circumstances both now and for eternity.[303]

3.3.4. DOCTRINAL AND PASTORAL DISCERNMENT, "Do not believe every spirit but test the spirits to see whether they are from God, because false prophets have gone out in the world" (1Jn 4:1).

---

[301] Ibid., 57.
[302] James Cochrane quoted in Stan Chu Ilo, "Searching for Healing in a Miraculous Stream," 57.
[303] Devison Telen Banda, "Jesus the Healer" *In Search of Health and Wealth: The Prosperity Gospel in Africa, Reformed Perspective,* ed. Hermen Kroesbergen (Eugene, OR: Wipf & Stock Publishers), 56.

Doctrinal and pastoral discernment supposes the discernment of spirit and constant prayer, to work and experience with prudence. The grace of God directs us to good, to truth, to humility, to obedience, to discretion, to simplicity, to truthful freedom, accepting with joy what we receive. Besides discerning spirits which has been proposed by Saint Ignatius of Loyola (which would need a broad elaboration beyond our work), we highlight here a pastoral and moral discernment: the capacity to differentiate reality from fiction, truth from falsity, good from evil, God from Devil, normal from paranormal phenomena.

As Nestor Salumu Ndalibandu rightly proposes, in the light of prevalent doctrinal and pastoral deviations and abuses observed in the lives of the faithful in some African Churches, moral and theological discernment is needed. It would examine the popular religiosity well-known in Sub-Saharan Africa, sensational liturgies; prosperity gospel about immediacy of health, wealth and salvation; superstitions, delusions, trances, visions, magical and symbolic images and positive relationships with the divine, as well as the traditional belief in witchcraft that reflect obscurantism, fundamentalism, and fatalism.[304] Indeed, there are risks of deviation for those who serve in the ministry of healing and exorcism due to lack of pastoral and doctrinal discernment. Pastoral authority must be firm and competent, holding the position of our mother Church with vigilance, attentiveness, tolerance, and coherence. *The Catechism of the Catholic* Church emphasizes the need for a catechesis that considers the forms of devotion among the faithful. [305]

As Ndalibandu clarifies, the insistence of the *Catechism of the Catholic Church* responds to the need of doctrinal discernment in relation to different pastoral practices. This implies lucidity and the concern of those holding the gift of healing, the reason for the phenomena in question through an analysis of information provided by the African mindset vis-à-vis Western thought. In this perspective, it would be disastrous to abruptly embrace what could be known as a charism of healing without a deep social and pastoral analysis in relation to the doctrine of the Church. Here the Church needs to face a double trend: On the one hand, the denial of existence of the demon, accompanied by an explanation of the phenomenon of possession as psychological crisis. On the other hand, seeing the demon everywhere and making it even responsible for all problems.

---

[304] Nestor Salumu Ndalibandu, *Les Prières d'Exorcismes et de Gurison dans l'Eglise Catholique en Afrique: Lecture Theologique et Pastorale* (Paris: L'Harmattan, 2017), 66.
[305] *Cathechism of The Catholic Church*, 81.

Aware of the issue, Pope Francis encourages the pastoral and pastoral *metanoia* in a certain openness to the real problems of the faithful. As Pope says:

> I would make it clear that not all discussion of doctrinal, in moral or pastoral issues need to be settled by interventions of the magisterium. Unity in teaching and practices is certainly necessary in the Church, but that does not preclude various ways of some aspects of that teaching and drawing some consequences from it. This will be always the case as the Spirit guides us to the entire truth (Jn 16:13), until he leads us fully into the mystery of Christ and enables us to see everything as he does. Each country and region, moreover, can seek solutions better suited to its culture and sensitive to its traditions and local needs. For cultures are in fact quite diverse, and every general principle…needs to be inculturated if it is to be respected and applied.[306]

CONCLUSION

In the light of what we have discussed in this third chapter on the search for an Effective Faith-Healing Ministry three major points needs to be emphasized.

First, we are called to reconsider Christ's preferential option for the poor. This entails active compassion and solidary efforts to effectively assist the last, the least, the mentally ill, the socially and physically broken and forgotten. It necessarily involves dismantling structural violence that fosters poverty, the culture-medium of many diseases.

Second, there is an urgency to adopt the art of accompaniment that uncovers the hidden wounds of people in the search for healing. The church with her ordinary ministers, priests, and pastors, as well as extraordinary ministers are, as Pope Francis says, "to remove their sandals" and reach out to people in dire need on the African continent. Although the logic of faith-healing remains problematic to many scholars, the choices that people make in joining healing crusades, or assemblies, their frequency at healing sites such as water streams, and deserted areas, should be an opportunity to provide better health care to people. It shows their quest for health and healing, and the Church is invited to meet people where they are and bring to them *shalom*: health and salvation.

---

[306] Pope Francis, *Amoris Laetitia*, no. 3.

Third, the search for health and healing in Africa needs to be addressed within a biomedical-social theological perspective. This entails bringing together medical researchers, policy makers, physicians, health officers, theologians, and scholars from multi-disciplinary fields. It must be done by engaging the teaching of the Church which is the mystical body of Christ who loves, cares, and came in the world that we may have life and have it abundantly. (Jn 10:10).

General Conclusion

To conclude this book, we hold that the realities lived in sub-Saharan Africa in matters of spiritual healing invite a pastoral and scientific commitment at the level of Catholic theology in dialogue with social and biomedical sciences. The important contribution of this book has been to call attention to the prevalence faith-healing experiences in Africa through a dialectical hermeneutic of ancestral beliefs and into the current Christian practices, specifically expressed in the life and the booming ministries of Catholic faith-healers.

Jean Marc Ela's criticism to theologians and to African clergy is in order: "Doing theology is no longer an academic exercise, but a spiritual adventure. This is the reason why the health situation in the villages and slums of Africa does not allow African theologians "shutting their eyes and drifting off to sleep with the purring of a clear conscience."[307] The health crisis calls theologians to be awaken and speak out.

Thus, one could restate the question raised in the first chapter: What is our take off in matters of ancestral practices which are still prevalent in today's Christian narratives? How do we regard rituals of possession, consultation of the mediums and diviners, traditional exorcisms, devil possession, levitation, paranormal phenomena? Could we hold that all these cases are unreal and irrational? Could we say that spiritual healing is ineffective, and that is all about placebo and autosuggestion? If that is the case, why are there sick people abandoned by contemporary biomedicine and psychiatric hospitals?

As Nathan has observed, there are an increasing number of untreated patients today. Even more unfortunate, these sick people are abandoned by all. Forgotten by politicians, physicians, biomedical researchers, they do not represent a rewarding research group. It becomes even more challenging when these patients refuse what they are asked to do. They are thus deserted, forgotten.[308] These desperate patients unveil our broken humanity. They show a deeply wounded society which we need thorough discernment and integral healing. We observed the persistence of beliefs of evil powers, belief in the power of ancestors (such as Lyangombe), belief in the psychosis of witchcraft and the control of evil spirits, fetishisms, misfortunes, toxic fears, religious manipulations, exploitation of the common good, misery of the public, as well as ignorance and illiteracy which foster belief in spirits. The book however

---

[307] Jean-Marc Ela, *My Faith as an African*, 180.
[308] Tobie Nathan, *L'Influence Qui Géurit* (Paris: Odile, 1994), 22.

opposes exaggerated belief in spirits. Too much belief on supernatural phenomenon can paralyze integral development and the improvement of living conditions of the population. It can hinder cultural and biomedical progress. It is an alarming situation to be denounced, starting with Church leaders, parish priests, African bishops, Synods, the magisterium, philosophers, sociologists, historians, and African theologians.

The second chapter addressed the emergence of faith healing ministries in the post Vatican Council, calling the Church to rethink the ministry of the sick. The Church in Africa is still influential and has medical centers and large hospitals which need to be upgraded. The Church cannot just be satisfied on being called "a field hospital," it is also a healing mother, caring for its sick children. Furthermore, the Church needs to be an ambassador which compassionately and actively advocates of the behalf of the poor, by living out the preferential option for the poor, by accompanying various diseased and sick persons. The Church needs to embrace an in depth-theological-biosocial perspective that could help address health problems at political, social, spiritual, and biological level. It needs to implement the pastoral care of proximity by accompanying the victims of the normal and paranormal phenomena in African society by spiritual guidance, intercessions, and by upgrading medical facilities for biomedical treatment. We noticed skepticism and myths surround the ministries of healing and exorcism in African societies. Despite pressing demands and solicitations of exorcism on the ground, many dioceses do not set up this pastoral ministry. The quest for healing has a social and ecclesial consequence in the view of proselytism of new religious movements and the influence of traditional customs. The African bishops have come back to this issue several times during the debates of the synods, and today's Holy See, with prudence and discernment is always in favor to healing and exorcism in a clear manner. To this end, in the second chapter, we have discussed the Church's tradition and teaching on healing and exorcism and healing in early Christianity, before and after Vatican II. We have seen that the practices of exorcism are becoming a growing ministry in the contemporary Western and African Church. There has been change in modern times with enlightenment and rationalism which affected the church and society. It was necessary to wait for the post-conciliar period because of the aggiornamento and perspectives of the Second Vatican Council as the Church encouraged the exercise of the gifts and charisms from the Holy Spirit,[309] and the functioning of the ministry of exorcism and healing with very certain restrictive orientations.

Finally, our third chapter highlighted the criteria of discernment for an effective faith-healing ministry in Africa through the lens of Catholic social healing. The book invited to invest in the biomedical research and in the moral and intellectual discernment in the perspective of pastoral care of the sick. We hold that exorcism and healing can be performed, yet in respect of liturgical forms of prayers established by the Church. To be performed, a healing ministry in Africa must be approved by ecclesial authorities. Faith healing is part of the charism of the Spirit bestowed on the mystical body, the Church. Still these gifts and charisms are not given to angels or spirits, but to God's people. We need to receive them and administer them, for the edification of God's people. It is also to be known that it is not the minister who heals or exorcise but the power of Christ that operates through the minister. When the poor cries, God hears, treats, and heals them. This should be, for us, an unshakable foundation and inspiration that mobilizes our faith and reason to be healers not by mere prayers, but by prayers coupled with deeds, by putting the preferential agenda of the poor in their various forms in our political priorities and Church ministries, by becoming today's Christ who accompanies and cares for the sick, the spiritually and the physically broken, the least and the last.

---

[309] Ecumenical Council, Vatican II, *Presbyterorum Ordinis, paragraph 9, See also Apostolicam Actuasiatem, paragraph,3.*

REFERENCES

Acolatse. E. Esther, *Powers, Principalities and Spirit*. Grand Rapids, MI: Eerdmans, 2018.

Appiah K.A. *In My Father's House: Africa in Philosophy of Culture*. Oxford : Oxford University Press, 1992.

Awazi Benoit Mbambi Kungua, *De la Post Colonie à la Mondialisation Néolibérale, Radioscopie Ethique de la Crise Négro-Africaine*. Paris: L'Harmattan, 2011.

Barry L. Blackburn, "The Miracles of Jesus": *Cambridge Companion to Miracles*. Graham H. Twelftree. Cambridge—New York: Cambridge University Press, 2011.

Bediako Kwame, *Jesus in Africa*. Akropong-Akuapen, Ghana: Regnum Africa, 2000.

Benedict XVI, *Jesus of Nazareth*. New York—Berlin, Bloomsbury, 2007.

------------, *AfricaeMunus,* http://w2.vatican.va/content/benedict-xvi/en/apost_exhortations/documents/hf_ben-xvi_exh_20111119_africae-munus.html#III._The_world_of_health_care.

https://www.newtimes.co.rw/timestv/national-prayer-breakfast-speech-president-kagame.

Bolaji E. Iodowu, *African Traditional Religion*. Maryknoll, NY: Orbis Books, 1975.

Binagwaho Agnes et al, *The Lancet* https://www.thelancet.com/journals/lancet/article/PIIS0140-6736(17)31509-X/fulltext.

See https://cruxnow.com/global-church/2018/06/23/africa-needs-christian-unity-to-survive-being-half-dead-pope-says/

Bujo Bénézet, *Foundations of An African Ethic*. Freiburg: Crossroad Publishing Company, 2016.

----------, *Panorama des Théologies Négro-Africaines.* Paris: L'Harmattan, 2002.

Cazanave A. Piarrot, "*Pratiques Sorcellaires et Crises Politiques au Burundi*"

http://geographica.danslamarge.com/Pratiques-sorcellaires-et-crises.html

Cahill S. Lisa, "Aids, Justice and the Common Good" *Catholic Ethicists on HIV/AIDS Prevention*. ed. James F. Keenan, S.J. New York: Continuum, 2000.

Chu Ilo Stan, "The Church of Pope Francis: An Ecclesiology of Accountability," Agbonkianmeghe E. Orobator, ed. *The Church We Want: African Catholics Look to Vatican II*. Maryknoll, NY: Orbis Books, 2016.

---------, "Searching for Healing in a Miraculous Stream: The fate of God's People in Africa" ed. Stan Chu Ilo, *Wealth, Health, and Hope in African Christian Religion*. Lanham—London: Lexington Books, 2018.

Catholic Church, *Catechism of the Catholic Church*, 2nd ed. Rome: Libreria Editrice Vaticana, 2012.

Catholic Church, *Catechism of The Catholic Church*, Promulgated by Pope John Paul II, 2nd ed. Washington, D.C: United States Catholic Conference, 1997.

Certeau Michel de, *The Possession at Loudun*, Paris: Gallimard, 1990.

Ceruki, Colloque, *Ryangombe, Mythes et Rites*. Bukavu, Editions du Ceruki, 1979.

Chu Ilo Stan, ed., *Wealth, Health and Hope in African Christian Religion*. Lanham—London: Lexington, 2018.

Congregation of the Doctrine of Faith, *The Instruction on Prayers for Healing, September 14*, 2000.

Cox Harvey, *The Secular City*. Princeton, N.J: Princeton University, 1965.

------------, *Fire from Heaven*. London : Cassel, 1996.

Dom Gabriele Amorth, *Exorcisme et Psychiatrie*, Paris : Droguet et Ardent, 2002.

Dom Gabriel Amorth, *Un Exorciste raconte*. Paris: Edition du Rocher, 2010.

D.S. Edwards, *Afro-Christian Religion and Healing in Southern Africa*. Lewiston—Lampeter: The Edwin Mellen, 1988.

Dubost Michel Mgr, Lalane Stanislas Mgr, *Le Nouveau Théo: Encyclopedie Théologique Pour Tous*. Paris: Mame, 2009.

Ela Jean Marc, *My Faith as An African*, Maryknoll, NY: Orbis, 1989.

Eliade Mircea, *Chamanisme et les Techniques d'Extase*, Paris, Payot, 1968.

Ewusie R. Moses, *Practices of Power: Revisiting the Principalities and Powers in the Pauline Letters*. Minneapolis, M.N: Fortress Press, 2014.

Favret-Saada Jeanne, *Les mots, La mort, Les Sorts*, Paris : Gallimard, 1977.

Froc Isidor, *Exorcistes : Repères dans un Nouvel Age*, Paris : Plon/Mame, 1996.

Ferngreen B. Gary, *Medicine and Religion: A Historical Introduction.* Baltimore, MD: John Hopkins University, 2014.

Francis Pope, *Amoris Laetitia: Encyclical Letter.* Vatican: The Holy See, Vatican Website: Libreria Editrice Vaticana. https://w2.vatican.va/content/dam/francesco/pdf/apost_exhortations/documents/papa-francesco_esortazione-ap_20160319_amoris-laetitia_en.pdf.

Francis Pope, *The Church of Mercy: A Vision for the Church.* Chicago: Loyola Press, 2014.

Gunderson Gary R. and James R. Cochrane, *Religion and the Health of the Public: Shifting the Paradigm.* New York: Palgrave McMillan, 2012.

Gordon Conwell, *Christianity in Its Global Context* https://www.gordonconwell.edu/ockenga/research/documents/2ChristianityinitsGlobalContext.pdf

Hastings Adrian, *African Catholicism: Essays in Discovery,* London: SCM Press, 1989.

Hebga Pierre Meinrad "Le Mouvement Charismatique en Afrique" *Etudes* No.1 & 2 (1995).

-----------, *Sorcellerie et Prière de Délivrance. Reflexion sur Une Expérience.* Présence Africaine, 1968.

------------, *La Rationalité d'Un Discours Africain sur les Phenomenes Paranormaux.* Paris: L'Harmattan, 1998.

------------, *Emancipation d'Eglises Sous Tutelle: Essaie sur l'Ere Post-Missionaries,* Paris: Presence Africaine, 1976.

------------, *Le Concept de Métamorphoses d'Hommes en Animaux chez les Basa, Douala, Ewondo Bantu, Sud Cameroon,* Rennes: University de Rennes, 1968.

H. Robert Codrington, *The Melanesians.* Oxford: Orbis, 1975.

Harrington J. Daniel, *Jesus: A Historical Portrait.* Cincinnati, OH: St Anthony, 2007.

Hervieu-Leger Daniele, *Le Pèlerin et le Converti, La Religion en Mouvement,* Paris: Flammarion, 1999.

Heusch de Luc, *Le Rwanda et la Civilisation Interlacustre.* Brussels: Institut de Sociologie, 1966.

Huerbsch Bill, *The Art of Accompaniment.* New London, CT: Twenty-Third Publications, 2017.

Ikeobi G. C, "Healing and Exorcism in Africa" *Spiritus* 120, 1990.

International Catholic Association of Exorcists, http://icaoe.weebly.com/membership.html

http://www.pewforum.org/2017/04/05/the-changing-global-religious-landscape/

Janice Price, *World Shaped Mission: Reimagining Mission Today.* London: Church House, 2012.

John Chrisostome's Homilies, See https://www.rogerpearse.com/weblog/wp-content/uploads/2014/05/chrysostom-devil-bryson-2014.pdf.

John Paull II, Encyclical Letter, *Fides et Ration: On The Relationship between Faith and Reason.* Libreria Editrice Vaticana, 1998.

Karellissa V. Hartigan, *Performances and Cure. Drama and Healing in Ancient Greece and Contemporary America.* London—Sidney, Bloomsbury, 1988.

Kabiro wa Gatumu. *The Pauline Concept of Supernatural Powers: A Reading from an African Worldview.* Eugene, OR: Wipf & Stock, 2008.

Luneau René, *Paroles and Silences du Synode Africain,1989-1995,* Paris: Karthala, 1997.

Magesa Laurenti, *African Religion: The Moral Tradition of Abundant life.* Maryknoll, NY: Orbis, 1997.

Mbonimpa Melchior, *Guérison et Religion en Afrique.* Paris: Harmattan, 2012.

Mbiti John, *New Testament Eschatology in an African Background.* New York: Oxford Press, 1971.

------------ African Religion and Philosophy. Oxford: Heinemann, 1990.

Milingo Emmanuel, *The World in Between*, New York: Maryknoll,1984.

Midelfort H. C Eric, *Exorcism and Enlightenment: Johann Joseph Gassner and the Demons of Eighteenth-Century Germany,* New Haven and London: Yale University Press, 2005.

Mulago gwa Cikala, *La Religion Traditionnelle des Bantu et leur Vision du Monde*, 2ème ed. Kinshasa : Faculté de Théologie Catholique de Kinshasa, 1980.

Nathan Tobie, *L'Influence Qui Geurit*, Paris: Odile, 1994.

Neckebrouck Victor, *Paradoxes de l'Inculturation.* Leuven: Leuven University Press, 1994.

Nouwen J. M. Henri, *The Wounded Healer: Ministry in the Contemporary Society.* New York—Auckland: Doubleday, 1979.

Our Sunday's Visitor Catholic Encyclopedia, Peter M.J. Stravinskas, ed. (Huntington, IN: Our Sunday's Visitors Publishers, 1998.

Olupande Dorcas Akintunde "Women as Healers," *African Women, Religion, and Health,* Isabel Apawo Phiri, Sorojini Nadar (Maryknoll, NY:Orbis Book,2006.

Paul VI, *Presbyterorum Ordinis, Decree on The Ministry and the Life of Priests,* December 7, 1965.
http://www.vatican.va/archive/hist_councils/ii_vatican_council/documents/vat-ii_decree_19651207_presbyterorum-ordinis_en.html.

Perugia Del Paul, *Les Derniers Rois Mages, Récits Ethnologiques.* Paris: Gallimard, 1970.

Poucouta Paulin, *African Theology in the 21st Century: The Contribution of Pioneers,* ed. Bénézet Bujo. Nairobi, Kenya: Pauline Africa, 2003.

Pew Forum on Religion & Public life, *Islam and Christianity in sub-Saharan Africa*
http://www.pewresearch.org/wp-content/uploads/sites/7/2010/04/sub-saharan-africa-appendix-b.pdf.

-----------, *The Changing Global Religious Landscape*
http://www.pewforum.org/2017/04/05/the-changing-global-religious-landscape/

Pobee Samuel, "Africa's Search for Religious Human Rights Through Returning to Wells of Living Water" *Religious Human Rights in Global Perspective: Legal Perspectives.* ed. Johan D.van der Vyer and John Witte, Jr. The Hague--London: Martinus Nijhoff, 1996.

Pheage Tefo "Dying from Lack of Medicines" *African Renewal.* December - March 2017. Online https://www.un.org/africarenewal/magazine/december-2016-march-2017/dying-lack-medicines.

Rosny Eric de, *Healers in the Night.* Maryknoll, NY: Orbis, 1985.

Rugirangoga Ubald, *Travel Schedule* https://frubald.com/about/travel-schedule/

------------------------, *Forgiveness Makes You Free. Notre-Dame*: IN, Ave Maria Press, 2019.

----------------------, *The Center for the Secret of Peace.*
https://frubald.com/the-center-for-the-secret-of-peace/

San Martin, *Crux.* https://cruxnow.com/global-church/2018/06/23/africa-needs-christian-unity-to-survive-being-half-dead-pope-says/.

Sanctuaire Ruhango. https://www.sanctuaireruhango.info.

Salumu Nestor Ndalibandu, *Les Prières d'Exorcismes et de Guérison dans l'Eglise Catholique en Afrique: Lecture Théologique et Pastorale.* Paris: L'Harmattan, 2017.

Shimba Banza, *Comment Guérir par La Prière*. Kinshassa: Médiaspaul, 2005.

Smith J. Z., Scott Green William, eds. *The Harper Collins Dictionary of Religion*. San Francisco, CA:
Harper Collins Publishers, 1995.

Suchet Amiotte Laurent, *Un Ministère de Bricolage Rituel: Le Cas d'un Exorciste Diocesain*. Ethnologie Française, no.161, 2016.

Sobrino Jon, *Christ The Liberator*. Maryknoll, NY: Orbis, 2001.

Southern African Catholic Bishop's Conference, *Ancestor Religion and the Christian Faith:* Pastor Statement, 11August, 2006.

Telen Devison Banda, "Jesus the Healer" *In Search of Health and Wealth: The Prosperity Gospel in Africa, Reformed Perspective*, ed. Hermen Kroesbergen. Eugene, OR: Wipf & Stock Publishers, 2014.

Thomas Louis-Vincent, *Laissez Mon Peuple Aller! Eglise Africaine au-delà des Modèles?* Paris: Karthala, 1987.

Tournyol du Clos, *Le Combat Avancé de l'Eglise*. Canohès, France: L'Archistratège, 2012.

Udelhoven Bernhard, *Unseen World: Dealing with Spirits, Witchcraft, and Satanism* Lusaka, Zambia: FENZA, 2015.

United States Conference of Catholic Bishops. *Guidelines of Evaluating Reiki as an Alternatives Therapy*. http://www.usccb.org/_cs_upload/8092_1.pdf

Vincentian Retreat Center, http://www.vrcthika.org.

World Bank, *Ending Extreme Poverty: Progress, But Uneven and Slowing* https://openknowledge.worldbank.org/bitstream/handle/10986/30418/97814648 13306_Ch01.pdf.

World Health Organization, https://www.who.int/about/who-we-are/constitution.

Zahan Dominique, *Religion et Spiritualité et Pensée Africaine*, Paris: Payot, 1970.

www.ingramcontent.com/pod-product-compliance
Lightning Source LLC
Chambersburg PA
CBHW050602300426
44112CB00013B/2038